Library of
Davidson College

EUROPEAN DIRECT INVESTMENT IN THE U.S.A.
BEFORE WORLD WAR I

Also by Peter J. Buckley

THE FUTURE OF THE MULTINATIONAL ENTERPRISE
(with Mark Casson)
GOING INTERNATIONAL: THE EXPERIENCE OF SMALLER
COMPANIES OVERSEAS
(with Gerald D. Newbould and Jane Thurwell)

EUROPEAN DIRECT INVESTMENT IN THE U.S.A. BEFORE WORLD WAR I

Peter J. Buckley
and
Brian R. Roberts

St. Martin's Press   New York

© Peter J. Buckley and Brian R. Roberts 1982

All rights reserved. For information, write:
St. Martin's Press, Inc., 175 Fifth Avenue, New York, NY 10010
Printed in Hong Kong
First published in the United States of America in 1982

ISBN 0-312-26940-4

Library of Congress Cataloging in Publication Data

Buckley, Peter J.   1949–
  European direct investment in the U.S.A. before
World War I.

  Bibliography: p.
  Includes index.
   1. Investments, European – United States–History.
2. Investments, Foreign–United States–History.
I. Roberts, Brian R., joint author.   II. Title.
HG4910.B83   1981   332.6′734′073   80–20511
ISBN 0-312-26940-4

Instead of being viewed as a rival ... [foreign capital] ... ought to be considered as a most valuable luxury, conducing to put in motion a greater quantity of productive labor and a greater proportion of useful enterprises, than could exist without it.

> Alexander Hamilton,
> First Secretary of the U.S. Treasury,
> *Report to Congress on Manufactures,* 1791

In modern speculation
Your language you must choose.
It's an 'investment' if you win
But 'gambling' if you lose.

Anglo-Colorado Mining Guide, VI (28 November, 1903)

Contents

List of Tables x

Preface xii

Acknowledgements xiii

1 DIRECT INVESTMENT 1

    1.1 Introduction 1
    1.2 Direct versus portfolio investment 1
    1.3 Syndicate investment and its relationship to portfolio investment 4
    1.4 Motives for direct foreign investment 5
    1.5 Direct investment and the imperfect market 7
    1.6 Internalisation of markets and the growth of firms 8
    1.7 Summary 9

2 A PRELIMINARY ANALYSIS OF DIRECT INVESTMENT IN THE U.S.A. 1870–1914 11

    2.1 Introduction 11
    2.2 The importance of the U.K. 12
    2.3 The continental European countries 16
    2.4 The cyclical nature of the investment 18
    2.5 Summary 19

3 THE HISTORICAL BACKGROUND TO FOREIGN INVESTMENT IN THE U.S.A. 20

    3.1 Introduction 20
    3.2 Colonial times to 1800 20

3.3	1800 to the Civil War	22
3.4	The Civil War to World War I	24
3.5	The importance of innovations and their origins	30
3.6	The U.S. economy in 1914	32
3.7	Previous investigations of European direct investments	33
3.8	Summary	42

4 A REVIEW BY INDUSTRY OF THE AREAS WHERE DIRECT INVESTMENT OCCURRED 1870–1917   43

4.1	Introduction	43
4.2	The chemical and dyestuffs industries	44
4.3	The textile industry	47
4.4	The oil industry	50
4.5	The brewing and liquor industry	53
4.6	The mining and allied industries	56
4.7	The land development industry	59
4.8	The flour-milling industry	63
4.9	The tobacco industry	64
4.10	The metal industry	65
4.11	The tin-plate industry	67
4.12	The silk industry	67
4.13	The electrical industry	67
4.14	The automobile industry	68
4.15	The railway industry	69
4.16	Finance, mortgage, insurance and banking companies	70
4.17	Other industries	73
4.18	Conclusion	82

5 EIGHT CASE HISTORIES   85

5.1	Introduction	85
5.2	Lever Brothers (U.K.)	86
5.3	Courtaulds Ltd (U.K.)	93
5.4	Royal Dutch Shell (Holland/U.K.)	95
5.5	Nobel and the Nobel Explosives Trust Company (Sweden/U.K./Germany)	100
5.6	Fiat (Italy)	103
5.7	Solvay et Cie (Belgium)	105

5.8	The Anglo-Swiss Condensed Milk Company and Henri Nestlé (Switzerland)	107
5.9	Siemens & Halske and A.E.G. (Germany)	112
5.10	Summary and conclusion	115

6 **CONCLUSION** 119

6.1	General	119
6.2	The impact of European direct investment on the development of the U.S.A.	121
6.3	Aftermath of World War I	123
6.4	Conclusion	128

Notes and References   130

Bibliography   140

Subject and Name Index   147

Company Name Index   153

List of Tables

2.1	European countries' shares in the total world foreign investment in 1913	12
2.2	U.K. share of total foreign investment in the U.S.A. between 1870 and 1914	13
2.3	Book value of foreign countries' direct investment in the U.S.A. in 1914	14
2.4	Lewis's sectoral breakdown of foreign direct investment in the U.S.A. before World War I	15
2.5	German-owned companies founded before 1899 still operating in 1914	17
3.1	Some significant European inventions, 1864–1914	31
3.2	Population and immigration in the U.S.A., 1800–1920	32
3.3	Total and per capita G.N.P. of the U.S.A., 1869–1921	33
3.4	Number of continental European parent systems with U.S. subsidiaries in 1913 by country	34
3.5	Location of foreign manufacturing of selected continental European companies about 1914	35
3.6	U.K. companies with U.S.A. manufacturing subsidiaries before 1914	36
3.7	U.K. companies with 'outpost' manufacturing facilities in the U.S. before 1914	37
3.8	European companies operating direct investments in the U.S.A. pre-World War I	38
4.1	Foreign-owned oil companies in the U.S.A., 1914 and 1919	52
4.2	Foreign-owned breweries in the U.S.A., 1914 and 1919	55
4.3	Foreign-owned mining companies in the U.S.A., 1914 and 1919	58
4.4	Foreign-owned land companies in the U.S.A., 1914 and 1919	60
4.5	Foreign-owned cattle companies in the U.S.A., 1914 and 1919	61
4.6	Foreign-owned mortgage and finance companies in the U.S.A. 1914 and 1919	71
4.7	Foreign-owned industrial companies in the U.S.A., 1914 and 1919	81
5.1	Countries of origin of the companies selected	86

5.2	Lever Brothers' Company employees: Cambridge office and factory	90
5.3	Lever Brothers' new overseas factories established between 1898 and 1913	91
5.4	Data on Shell's activities in the U.S.A., 1912–20	99
5.5	Number of European cars imported into the U.S.A. in 1907	103
5.6	Anglo-Swiss and Nestlé's overseas factories at the time of their merger in 1905	110
5.7	Summary of case histories	116
6.1	An estimate of the relative importance of foreign direct investment in the U.S.A., 1914 and 1919	122
6.2	Net asset position of the U.S.A., 1869–1935	124
6.3	Distribution of British foreign investments, 1913 and 1930	126
6.4	Book value of foreign countries' direct investments in the U.S.A. in 1914 and 1919	127

FIGURE

3.1	Principal Marconi enterprises, 1897–1917	40

Preface

The humble origins of the huge multinational companies of today often come as a shock. To examine the early struggles of such companies as Nestlé, I.C.I., Unilever and Siemens is a salutary lesson in business history. Moreover, it is fascinating to examine 'what might have been' in terms of those companies which failed to survive under the pressures which forged today's giants.

It is also of great relevance to examine the period 1870–1917 as an early stage of the development of international investment and to test the explanatory power of modern theories in a world economy very different from that of today.

These reasons provided the initial motivation for the present study of European direct investment in the U.S.A., 1870–1917. There is currently a re-examination of early foreign investment being undertaken, which suggests that direct investment was an important component of total foreign investment even before World War I. Our research tends to support this contention.

The study of the period presents great difficulties of data availability. Few contemporary or early twentieth-century writers focused on international direct investment, for this period was the golden age of the migration of portfolio capital and of labour, particularly to the regions of recent settlement. Records of many firms have been misplaced or destroyed – and business history has not always been seen as a fruitful area of research, although thankfully this now seems to have changed. Consequently, we have frequently had to rely on one source for quite considerable areas of information, and it has often not been possible to check assertions from original sources.

Bradford
March 1980

P. J. B.
B. R. R.

Acknowledgements

The authors and publishers wish to thank the following for permission to reproduce copyright material: George Allen & Unwin Ltd and Humanities Press Inc. for the tables from *Studies in International Investment* by John H. Dunning; B. T. Batsford for a table from *FIAT* by Michael Sedgwick; Brookings Institution for the tables and the material from *America's Stake in International Investments* by Cleona Lewis, copyright © Brookings Institution; *Business History Review* for the tables which first appeared as pp. 316–17 and 324 in 'The Origins of British Based Multinational Manufacturing Enterprises' by John M. Stopford, *Business History Review*, vol. 48, no. 3; Cambridge University Press for the table from *An Economic Background to Munich* by Alice Teichova; Harper & Row Inc. for the tables from *The European Multinationals* by L. Franko (1976); and the Shell Oil Company for the material from *Enterprise in Oil* by Kendall Beaton.

We are particularly grateful for assistance from Gordon A. Burnett (Vice-President, Coats & Clark Inc.), C. J. Cornwall (Company Secretary, Courtaulds Ltd), J. D. Kerr (Company Secretary, Unilever Ltd), Maureen Staniforth and Jillian Gunn (Unilever Information Library), G. MacFarlane (Company Secretary, Bryant & May Ltd), Dr Schoen (Werner-von-Siemens Institute für Geschichte des Hauses Siemens), E. Henry (Secretary General, Nestlé S.A.), A. F. Peters (Shell Centre, London), J. Boyajian (Shell Oil Company, U.S.A.), Mr D. Clifford (Company Secretary, Reckitt & Colman Ltd), Mr D. M. Pearson (Chairman, BBA Group Ltd), and many others who have helped with information.

We would also like to thank Neil Hunter, Librarian, and the staff of the University of Bradford Management Centre Library for their kind and most efficient help. Neil Hunter also prepared the index. Thanks are also due to Mrs Sylvia Ashdown, Mrs Dorothy Dufaux and Mrs Sandra Dwyer for their careful and speedy typing of drafts of the book. Finally, we would like to thank Dr Michael Brooke, U.M.I.S.T., and Dr Paul Shorter for their comments on previous drafts of this book, and Patrick Artisien for help in translations.

As always, final responsibility for what appears in the pages following rests solely with the authors.

Bradford
March 1980

P. J. B.
B. R. R.

1 Direct Investment

1.1 INTRODUCTION

This book examines European direct investment in the United States of America (U.S.A.) in the period before World War I.* Our concerns are to examine the extent and nature of such investment; to assess the impact the investment had on the development of the economy of the U.S.A. and to provide explanations of this early direct investment in the light of the modern theories of international business. Our major concern is manufacturing industry but we shall also follow European capital into agriculture, extraction and mining, and service industries such as insurance and banking. No attempt is made to assess the impact of such investment on the source economies.

We begin by examining the difference between portfolio and direct foreign investment (Section 1.2). In Section 1.3 we examine syndicate investment, which was an important component of foreign investment 1870–1917 but which has since drastically declined. Section 1.4 deals with the range of motives which can lead a company to make a foreign direct investment, and Section 1.5 examines the relationship between the foreign investment decision and the existence of market imperfections. In Section 1.6 we introduce the role of growth by internalisation of markets and its possible relevance to direct foreign investment in the U.S.A. before 1917.

1.2 DIRECT VERSUS PORTFOLIO INVESTMENT

The features which distinguish direct from portfolio investment can be usefully explained by their arrangement into five parts:

---

*Although World War I began in Europe in July and August 1914 (Britain declared war on Germany on 4 August 1914), the U.S.A. entered the War on 6 April 1917. We have therefore used 1914 for European events, 1917 for the U.S.A. when referring to the end of our period of investigation.

(1) The fundamental aspect of direct as opposed to portfolio investment is that the investor purchases the power to exert some kind of control over the management of the investment and it therefore implies that something other than capital alone is involved. This can be items such as managerial and technical capability or marketing knowledge. This power of control will vary with the distribution of the equity in the company in question. The standard explanation of this is that an investor holding 30 per cent of the voting equity in a company, where no other investor holds more than 10 per cent, is more likely to be able to exercise control, in spite of his minority holding, than he would be if he held 49 per cent with the other 51 per cent in one person's or company's hands.

(2) Direct investment usually involves the movement of factors other than capital, as mentioned in (1) above.

(3) There is a fundamental difference in the ultimate target for direct investment and that for portfolio. Portfolio capital will tend to move to sectors in the foreign country that have an advantage over their counterparts in the same country.[1] This advantage will be reflected by the superior profit or return on investment record of the foreign companies. Exactly the opposite is likely to occur with direct investment in that it will often flow to companies in an industry where the source country had the advantage but where this advantage can be transferred to the foreign country to its ultimate gain. However, although this may be typical of much of today's foreign direct investment, it will be seen that the majority of cases between 1870 and 1917 were instigated by the imposition of tariffs by the U.S.A. and the consequent attempt by European companies to try to avoid the loss of their exports.

(4) The vast majority of portfolio investment is carried out by individuals or institutions, not companies. They tend to invest in foreign individuals and institutions through the foreign capital market mechanism. In the case of foreign direct investment, it is usually carried out by companies. It may involve the purchase of all or part of a foreign company involving a change of ownership or, alternatively, it may involve the setting up of an entirely new plant overseas in the form of a vertical or horizontal but still geographical extension of the firm's activities. This may be for reasons other than immediate profit maximisation, i.e. the safeguarding of a source of raw material or, as has been discussed in (3), the threat to an export trade and consequential loss to the firm.

(5) As mentioned by Kindleberger,[2] direct investment need not involve a flow of capital from one country to another at all. Economists used to

think of direct investment as an international movement of capital which could take place in a variety of forms, for example, through the issue of new securities usually in the form of bonds, through the purchase and sale of existing stocks and bonds through security exchanges or through a variety of short-term credit instruments and forms. The only difference that the economists would concede to was that direct investment was accompanied by varying degrees of control plus the movement of management and technology. However, it became evident that in certain cases, equity was gained in exchange for knowledge of patents or technology or in exchange for machinery, and that in other cases, the investors did not take any money abroad with them but borrowed it on the local market of the country in question. A third case occurred when the investing company already had a subsidiary abroad and, rather than repatriating the profits, it was reinvesting them in the host country. This reinvestment could be in the subsidiary itself in the form of expansion or as a stake in some other new or existing company. In either event, the non-repatriation of the profits represented a net increase in the foreign direct investment of the company in question. In none of these cases would there have been any actual flow of capital from one country to another.

A special type of foreign investment is noted by Stopford[3] as 'expatriate' investment. This form of investment occurs where an entrepreneur migrates and starts a firm in his new homeland, financed by capital from his old homeland. Management control is not exercised from the source country and such investments soon become indigenous to the host country. The importance of this form of investment can be readily appreciated in the areas of new settlement. Such investment is not direct foreign investment, however, and is excluded from this work, although it is acknowledged, particularly in the earliest period covered here, that there is often a thin line (bound up with decisions on the locus of control) between 'expatriate' and direct investment.

Concerning the distinction (arbitrary in many cases) between direct and portfolio investment, it should be noted, following Svedberg,[4] that early investigators often used a two-fold distinction including the control factor and the medium through which the investment took place — portfolio investment — being regarded as that which passed through the stock exchange rather than as an intra-firm investment flow. This and other factors may have led to underestimation of the direct component of international investment pre-1917, a contention which will be looked at again.

1.3 SYNDICATE INVESTMENT AND ITS RELATIONSHIP TO PORTFOLIO INVESTMENT

From the discussion in Section 1.2 it is apparent that there is a distinct analytical difference between direct and portfolio investment, but there is a further category of investment identified by Coram[5] as syndicate investment where the difference is less distinct.

Syndicate investment was a feature of the period under discussion and particularly with regard to British foreign investment in the U.S.A. The idea came about as a direct result of the frequent losses being made by private U.K. portfolio investors who were suffering from the trade depression in the U.S.A. in the 1870s which was forcing many companies into bankruptcy.

The idea was that if a group of individuals combined their available capital and invested it in the form of a syndicate, the amount available for investment could be raised to a level high enough to enable either partial or complete control to be purchased. It was thought that if some form of control over the investments had been obtained, it would greatly improve the chances of the success of the investment.

Although this idea seemed sound in theory and was adopted by many groups of individuals, in practice it was not so good. Probably the best example of the difficulties encountered was the syndicate investment in the U.S. brewing industry which is described in more detail in Chapter 4. One of the reasons for the general failure of syndicates was their inability to make quick and correct decisions. Any decisions reached would only be as a result of meetings and discussions and would almost invariably be compromises because of the diverse interests and opinions of the syndicate members. In reality, although the syndicate as a whole could exercise control, in practice the individuals involved could not. In most cases their investments were to all intents and purposes, portfolio.

In addition to the fact that control exercised by syndicates was usually ineffective when compared with that exercised by the board of directors of a company who usually have similar interests, it is also impossible to distinguish quantitatively between portfolio and syndicate investments in the various statistics available. For these two reasons, syndicate investment in this work will be considered much more akin to portfolio investment than to direct investment and will therefore be treated as part of the former.

1.4 MOTIVES FOR DIRECT FOREIGN INVESTMENT

Having defined what is meant by direct investment and how it differs from portfolio investment, it is important to identify as many reasons as possible why a company should decide to invest abroad and why it should choose to make a direct rather than portfolio investment. Generally companies do not make portfolio investments because they can make a higher return on any spare capital they may have by using it in conjunction with the knowledge of technology, marketing and management that they already have (i.e., it is more profitable to internalise the advantage within the firm rather than sell it — perhaps in the form of a licence). This knowledge may well be the product of a previous investment. In a few cases the company may have a certain amount of excess capital but only for a limited period. Here, the company may well make a portfolio investment of limited duration. The vast majority of portfolio investments are made by institutions and individuals who do not have the company's specialised knowledge.

Brooke and Remmers[6] have identified a comprehensive list of the possible motives behind a company's foreign investment decision. These they arranged under three main headings: defensive strategies; aggressive or attacking strategies and other pressures.

Defensive strategies include the following situations where the company was operating abroad to defend its existing business:

(1) The situation where the company found its export trade to a specific country threatened by that country's imposition of tariffs, import controls or quotas, or its legislation against monopolies or trade agreements such as cartels.
(2) The situation where public or government opinion was in favour of local production of the product in question rather than importing it, or where other forms of nationalism were apparent.
(3) The situation where the cost of transport and/or delays in transport were threatening exports.
(4) The situation where problems with agents or licensees were threatening sales in the overseas markets.
(5) The situation where unsatisfactory after-sales servicing or other technical problems might prejudice either repeat or new sales.
(6) The situation where protection of patents in the overseas market was necessary.

(7) The necessity to ensure supplies of raw materials or components where perhaps they were only obtainable in particular countries.
(8) The necessity to invest abroad as a result of a similar decision taken by competitors or possibly by suppliers or customers.
(9) The necessity to protect shareholders from recessions at home by spreading the company's activities internationally or by diversifying the product group which in turn might involve geographical expansion.

Aggressive strategies were considered to be those where the following situations arose:

(1) The situation where certain resources were underemployed at home and could be profitably employed overseas. These resources were subdivided into capital equipment, personnel and know-how.
(2) The situation where the most effective use of existing or future opportunities could be made by the development of an international strategy.
(3) The necessity to gain access to foreign knowledge or methods.
(4) The necessity for expansion abroad where this was no longer possible at home or where it avoided domestic constraints.

Other pressures were the last category of motives. Examples of these were:

(1) The situation where government policies created a significant influence over the company by general encouragement to foreign investment in their country; tax concessions; cheap loans; grants or guarantees or concessionary buildings.
(2) The situation where other companies exerted an influence, for example, through an approach to know-how.
(3) The situation where internal pressure groups with particular expertise and in favour of overseas investment, could exert their influence over the company.

Taken together the three categories represent a very exhaustive identification of possible motives that could lead a company to the decision to invest abroad. There is, however, a distinction between the motive leading a company to make a direct investment and the company's objectives once it has done so. Any company undertaking a foreign direct investment will certainly do so to advance its own interests, but there may be several objectives common to all direct investment decisions and these may carry different weights with different companies. In the many cases where the capital involved in the foreign investment is only a small proportion of the firm's total capital, the management may be prepared to take a larger gamble with it than they would with the capital involved at home. In general, this is not the case today although it might have been in the years 1870–1917. Certainly firms like Lever Brothers and the Anglo-Swiss Condensed Milk Company (see Chapter 5) continued to expand in the U.S.A. although they failed to make a worthwhile return both before and after the expansion. In these two cases, the firms' main objective was to establish a name and product in the market rather than the maximisation of profits. In both cases, the motive behind the move to foreign production was the increasing difficulty in supplying the U.S. market from Europe, linked with the desire to retain that market once it had been captured.

1.5 DIRECT INVESTMENT AND THE IMPERFECT MARKET

The Brooke and Remmers aggressive strategies listed in Section 1.4 can be thought of as the optimum use of an advantage that a company may have over its competitors. This advantage is at the core of the Hymer–Kindleberger theory of direct foreign investment.[7]

The Hymer–Kindleberger theory states that the company must earn a higher rate of return abroad to compensate for the risks and extra cost of operating in a different legal and political environment, often at a considerable distance from the source country. The company must also earn a higher rate of return than the local firms operating in the same industry. If this was not the case, the money would simply flow to the local firms through the normal capital markets. The firm must therefore have an advantage which can fairly readily be transferred abroad, but at the same time cannot be acquired by the local firms. For all these conditions to be met the international market for technology, management, labour skills, components and other inputs must be imperfect.

In relation to this question of higher rate of return and risk, Edelstein states in his conclusion:

> ... It is therefore a tentative hypothesis of this study that the critical element in the isolation of home markets from the markets for some overseas assets was the higher return-risk characteristics of the latter, not the fact of their overseas origin and in the latter half of our period 1870–1913, the high return-risk securities of the newly emergent large-

scale domestic corporations contributed to a lessening of this type of isolation.[8]

Although Edelstein is referring to portfolio investment, his comments apply to direct investment as well. International direct investment is therefore most likely to occur where the market knowledge is imperfect and where it is not profitable to exploit the advantage by other means, e.g., licensing, franchising or exporting. Where the extra costs of exporting such as distribution and marketing added to the basic cost of the goods in the home country are more than the cost of production abroad, it will pay to produce abroad.

If the company is having problems maintaining or increasing its level of exports because of local government tariffs, communal customs, union tariffs or other forms of import control, this fact will be accentuated. This was undoubtedly true in the 1870–1917 period which was one of exceptionally high tariffs in the U.S.A. The Morill Act of 1861 meant that by 1864 average duty on goods coming into the U.S.A. was 47.1 per cent. This rose to 49.5 per cent after the McKinley tariff of 1891 and finally to 57 per cent after the Dingley tariff of 1897.[9] This rate was the highest ever imposed and was instituted primarily to protect developing U.S. industry. Many plausible reasons for the imposition of tariffs have been given by the governments involved but they formed an important incentive to foreign investments, for European firms were discouraged from exporting to the U.S.A. Another common contributor to market imperfections, particularly in the U.S.A., was the trust system. It is perhaps ironic that the U.S.A., where public opinion has always been against the formation of trusts, should have maintained such a high level of tariffs over the years.[10]

1.6 INTERNALISATION OF MARKETS AND THE GROWTH OF FIRMS

The theme of market imperfections as a major stimulus to foreign direct investment is taken further in the modern general theory of direct investment. The theory points to the operation of intra-firm 'internal' markets as an alternative to the use of external markets. The choice facing a firm is to use the external market, i.e. to buy from outside suppliers, or to carry out the process itself. Thus, the size and spread of the firm is determined by its decision on the internalisation of the various markets it faces in final and intermediate goods, raw materials and factors of production. Firms grow by replacing the market — if the market in question is in raw materials or intermediate goods, then the firm becomes vertically integrated; if final goods markets are internalised, horizontal integration results. This explanation is combined with location theory elements (themselves affected by internalisation decisions) to explain the spread of multinational enterprises.[11]

Particularly strong incentives to internalise occur where unique assets, the products of research or organisational innovation are in the possession of individual firms. The existence of regional and national barriers to other forms of international operation (e.g. tariffs, local marketing preferences) increases the desire to internalise markets although a major disincentive to internalisation arises from the increased communication costs involved in the organisation of internal markets.

It has been suggested that before World War II the main incentives to internalisation internationally occurred in raw materials markets and that post-World War II investment has been largely in oligopolistic advantages arising from research-intensive product markets.[12] It does seem, however, that the role of innovation and 'exploiting patents' was an important motivation for European direct foreign investment even before World War I.[13] It is of great interest to discover if the modern theory can help explain this early period of foreign direct investment.

1.7 SUMMARY

Our main concern is the analysis of European direct investment in the U.S.A. A major distinguishing feature of direct investment is that it involves control from the source country. There is therefore an element of judgement in classifying investments into 'direct', portfolio, syndicate or expatriate. It is clear, however, that direct investment is analytically, if not always practically, a distinct type of investment which raises rather different issues from the others. The motives and effects of foreign control, the nature of decision-making exercised by foreign firms, the industrial implications and growth-stimulating aspects of European investment are all objects of investigation.

The modern literature on foreign direct investment examines the generation of internationally transferable assets (technology, marketing skills, capital market power among others) and their exploitation through the internalisation (and therefore intra-firm control) of markets. The standard theory of location of economic activity suggests that market growth, tariff barriers and the superior profitability of low-cost locations will combine with the above factors to encourage flows of direct investment rather than market servicing by exports.

A major point of interest is the extent to which these factors were operative in a very different world economy from today's — that existing before World War I.

2 A Preliminary Analysis of Direct Investment in the U.S.A. 1870–1914

2.1 INTRODUCTION

In many of the examples of foreign direct investment used in this book, it has been impossible to give a quantitative value. Frequently there are either no figures available or where there are the source of the capital is not known. It is, however, possible to give a fairly accurate appraisal of the overall investment situation regarding the flow of capital from Europe to the U.S.A. between 1870 and 1914 and to emphasise the major part that the U.K. played in this transfer of capital.

Nurske has stated that between the end of the American Civil War in 1865 and the start of World War I in 1914, approximately 60 million people from Europe emigrated to what he describes as the regions of recent settlement.[1] These were countries in the world's temperate latitudes such as Canada, Australia, New Zealand, South America and the U.S.A. These areas received nearly all of the U.K.'s emigrants and about two-thirds of all its capital exports.

The 50-year period from 1865 to 1914 saw the total world long-term investment rise from $4 billion to $44 billion. The magnitude of this is more apparent when it is considered that, in 1914, 91 per cent of the total world foreign investment from the first use of money to the present time, had taken place within the last 50 years.[2] In considering this period, particularly the investment in foreign manufacturing that occurred during it, a very complete appraisal of the situation up to 1914 can be made.

In Section 2.2 the importance of the U.K. is discussed and in Section 2.3 the part played by other European countries is examined. Finally, in Section 2.4 an explanation for the rise and fall in the amount of capital being transferred is given. This transfer flow was not a continuous steady flow but rather a series of periods of high activity followed by low activity, and this phenomenon must be examined.

2.2 THE IMPORTANCE OF THE U.K.

In 1900 the U.K. was by far the most important country in the capital exporting business, accounting for 75 per cent of all international capital movements. Although this importance began to decrease after 1900, in 1913 the U.K. still accounted for $18.0 billion or 40.9 per cent of the world total of $44 billion.[3] Table 2.1 shows that the next biggest foreign investor after the U.K. was France but with a total of less than half that of the U.K. Indeed, the total for the five other European countries together at $20.3 billion amounts to only slightly more than that of the U.K.

TABLE 2.1 European countries' shares in the total world foreign investment in 1913

Country	Total ($ billion)	Percentage of world total
France	9.0	20.4
Germany	5.8	13.2
Belgium, Switzerland, Holland	5.5	12.5
U.K.	18.0	40.9
U.S.A.*	3.5	8.0
Other countries	2.2	5.0

* The U.S.A.'s gross debits were $6.8 billion — 15.5 per cent of the world's international debt. She was thus a net debtor immediately prior to World War I.

Source: Dunning (1970), *Studies in International Investment*, George Allen & Unwin, p. 22.

Thomas found that in 1913 the gross debtor position of the U.S.A. was $6.8 billion or 15.5 per cent of the total world overseas investment at that time. He also found that in the period 1870–1914 between 55 and 60 per cent of the net foreign investment in the U.S.A. was contributed by the U.K.[4] Dunning has estimated that the U.K. share of the foreign investments in the U.S.A. fell from its peak of 90 per cent to 59 per cent by 1913. Table 2.2 shows the figure for other selected years.

Dunning has stated that in 1914 90 per cent of all international capital movements took the form of portfolio investment, and in addition he has said that the incentive for direct rather than portfolio investment has become more pronounced over the years because technological gaps between countries have become more pronounced and because technological advance has increasingly become the main determinant of a country's economic advancement.

This view, however, has been challenged and the suggestion made that before World War I direct investment accounted for a much higher proportion than previously thought. Svedberg[5] suggests four major reasons for the underestimation: First, a lack of empirical evidence; second, the definitional change — dropping the medium of investment as a discriminator increases the 'direct' proportion; third, the incomplete coverage of direct investment arising from the fact that smaller companies were ignored; and finally, the underestimation of the value of direct investment which is usually 'book value'. Svedberg suggests that the proportion of foreign investment which can properly be defined as direct in the underdeveloped countries 1913—14 was between 44 and 60 per cent. It has previously been acknowledged, however, that the U.S.A. was an exception because the direct component was higher than in other host countries.

TABLE 2.2 U.K Share of total foreign investment in the U.S.A. between 1870 and 1914

Year	Share (%)
1880	80
1899	72
1913	59

Source: Dunning (1970), pp. 178—81.

Certainly, the evidence available suggests that European direct investment has been underestimated, particularly in view of difficulties of valuing at anything other than book value and of obtaining full coverage, neither of which we have been able to fully overcome.

An indication of the diversity of the U.K. overseas investments and the percentage of her national income that they represented has been given by Dunning.[6] In 1913, 40 per cent of the British total foreign investment was in the railway industry which at that time was one of the most powerful initiators of growth; 30 per cent was in either government or municipal securities, 5 per cent was in public utilities, 15 per cent was in industry, finance or commerce, and the final 10 per cent was in the traditional investment areas of mineral and raw material exploitation.

Expressed as a percentage of her national income, the total U.K. overseas investment between 1870 and 1913 was 4 per cent, and if the years 1904 to 1913 are considered the figure is 7 per cent. However, what is even more incredible is that between 1870 and 1913 the overseas investment was 40 per cent of the total U.K. capital accumulation. Eighty-five per cent of all the U.K. investment overseas took the form of fixed interest-bearing securities channelled through a chain of specialist banking and issuing houses.

Direct investment

The reports of the Alien Property Custodian[7] give what is probably one of the more accurate pictures of the book value of foreign countries' direct investments in the U.S.A. at the outbreak of World War I. The Alien Property Custodian was a body set up to ascertain the extent of foreign-controlled companies in the U.S.A. with a view to seizing and disposing of those controlled by the enemies of the U.S.A.

According to Lewis, the Custodian defined control subjectively, judging each case on its merits as opposed to taking some arbitrary level of ownership of shares as being that at which control started. The figures arrived at are detailed in Table 2.3. Again, this shows the dominant position held by the U.K. in 1914 with just under 50 per cent of all foreign investment in the U.S.A. Total European direct investment can thus be estimated at over $1.1 billion.

Staley[8] has noted that in 1913, 20.3 per cent of all the U.K.'s international investment was in the U.S.A. but the only partial estimate of the value invested in each industrial sector in the U.S.A. is by Lewis, as shown in Table 2.4. Lewis's sectoral breakdown is of limited value because it is

TABLE 2.3 Book value of foreign countries' direct investment in the U.S.A. in 1914

Creditor country	$ million	Creditor country	$ million
U.K.	600	France	45
Germany	300	Austria–Hungary, Bulgaria, Turkey	30
Netherlands	135	All others*	50
Canada	132		
		TOTAL	1292

* Includes two sizeable Belgian investments and one Swiss as at 1 July 1914.
Source: Lewis (1938), p. 546.

TABLE 2.4 Lewis's sectoral breakdown of foreign direct investment in the U.S.A. before World War I

Sector	Estimate of direct investment amount	Nationality of ownership	Notes
1. Land-holding companies	$40 million 1914 $52 million at peak	Mostly British	Between 30 and 35 million acres owned by foreign firms for a period of a few months before World War I
2. Cattle companies	$5.9 million	British	Only two active at close of World War I ($2.9 million value)
3. Mining companies	'not less than $56 million' British $10.2 million French + one $7 million project 50% German-owned + small amount Belgian capital		—
4. Oil companies	$35 million (underestimate)		In 1922 investments of Shell alone $205 million
5. Breweries and liquor companies	$58 million nominal capital British $6 million German (underestimate)		—
6. Other foreign industrial companies	$36 million British $13 million French and Belgian German?		—
7. Mortgage companies	'At beginning of War foreign loans on American real estate probably aggregated not less than 200 to 250 million dollars'		—
8. Foreign-controlled railways	?	?	
9. Foreign-controlled banks	?	?	1934 First list of banks — 54 agencies $16.4 million deposits out of $50 billion total
10. Insurance	?	?	
TOTAL	Approx. $1.3 billion	?	
TOTAL EUROPEAN DIRECT INVESTMENT 1914	Approx. $1.1 billion	?	

Source: Derived from Lewis (1938), chapter 5.

incomplete. Notable omissions from Table 2.3 are the brewing and petroleum industries.

2.3 THE CONTINENTAL EUROPEAN COUNTRIES

Although there were some fairly substantial investments by continental European capitalists in the 1860s, particularly those by the Germans and Dutch, Dunning[9] states that the majority of this capital had been withdrawn by the end of the following decade at the time of the Franco-Prussian War. In later years France and Germany were to become important countries in the field of international investment but France never invested to any significant degree in the U.S.A., and by 1898 less than one-third of the total German overseas investment was in North and South America.[10]

One reason for the difference between the emphasis put on the U.S.A. by U.K. and continental European investors, other than the traditional and historical links between the U.S.A. and the U.K., was the role of the various national governments.[11] In the U.K. there was only the mildest government influence over the flow of capital which was very largely the product of the private enterprise sector, while in France and Germany foreign investments were undertaken largely to achieve national objectives and were therefore subject to a high level of government intervention.

Of the German total of $5.8 billion foreign investment (direct and portfolio) in 1913, only one-third (or about $2 billion) went to North and South America,[12] and allowing for the German influence in South America which was as strong as in the U.S.A. or Canada, probably less than $1 billion was invested in the U.S.A., of which $300 million is Lewis's estimate of direct investment. Table 2.5 shows that some German firms had valuable holdings even before 1900. (Note the importance of brewing, excluded from Lewis's estimates in Table 2.3).

The French record of relative disinterest in the U.S.A. was even more marked than the German. In 1900, out of the French total of Fr.28 billion only Fr.0.8 billion went to North America and in 1914 the position was Fr.2 billion out of a total of Fr.45 billion. In both cases North America includes Canada. When the French influence in Canada is considered then it is reasonable to assume that the U.S.A. would only have received a small part of what was already a relatively meagre French investment there.

In Table 2.3 the book values placed by the Alien Property Custodian on European countries' investments can be seen. At $300 million the German contribution is more than twice that of the Netherlands and over

TABLE 2.5 German-owned companies founded before 1899 still operating in 1914

Name of German-controlled company	Valuation and Notes	Date incorporated or acquired by German interests
American Metal Co. (Ltd)	Capitalised at $1 million in 1899	1887
Roessler & Hasslacher Chemical Co.	Capitalised at $1.3 million in 1915	1889
Peter Schoenhofer Brewing Co.	Capitalised at $3.0 million in 1889	1889
United States Brewing Co.	Capitalised at $5.5 million in 1889	1889
Botany Worsted Mills	—	1890
Merck and Co.	—	1891
German–American Lumber Co.	—	1894
Kny Scherer Corp.	Largest vendor of surgical equipment in the U.S.A. pre-1914. Bought by A.G.F.M.	1896
L. Vogelstein	An agency of Aron Hirsch & Son	1897
Hamburg–American Line Terminal & Navigation Co.	—	Before 1899

Source: Lewis (1938), p. 528, reporting estimates of N. T. Bacon (1900), 'American International Indebtedness', *Yale Review*, November 1900, pp. 265–85.

six times that of France, but only half that of the U.K. The sale of the assets of the 330 German firms involved in the U.S.A., not surprisingly, realised less than the book value. In fact, the figure was $275 million[13] but the figures do nonetheless give a good idea of the European countries' stakes in the U.S.A. relative to each other. To include portfolio investments in these figures would of course increase them dramatically, possibly by a factor of 10. Staley[14] has noted that, in 1913, Germany's holdings in the U.S.A and Canada together represented 15.7 per cent of her total foreign investments with a respective figure for France of 2.2 per cent. The U.K. figure for the U.S.A. alone was 20.3 per cent.

2.4 THE CYCLICAL NATURE OF THE INVESTMENT

The early 1870s were particularly busy years as far as U.K. investment in the U.S.A. was concerned and Dunning[15] has identified several reasons for this:

(1) The return to normality in the U.S.A. after the Civil War and the resulting resurgence of business activity. A major contributor was the new period of U.S. railway growth which accounted for 40 per cent of all the securities offered by private U.K. companies operating abroad at that time.
(2) The comparatively bargain prices at which U.S. government bonds were available to the U.K. public in the aftermath of the Civil War.
(3) The renewed interest in mining ventures in the U.S.A. between 1870 and 1873 saw the formation of 67 U.K. companies for prospecting in the Rocky Mountains.

This last reason would appear to tie up nicely with the work of North,[16] who identified a succession of peaks and troughs in the U.S. net capital movements in the years in question. He identified the years 1910, 1888 and 1872 as peak years with net inflows of capital at $51.1 million, $285 million and $224.8 million respectively. In addition, he identified the years 1900, 1878 and 1858 as trough years with net outflows of capital at $296.4 million, $161.9 million and $231 million respectively.

Dunning[17] has identified the period 1863—70 as one of rapid internal growth in the U.S.A. and considerable foreign investment mainly in federal and state bonds and the railroads. The U.S. balance of payments during this period was unfavourable. From the peak of expansion in 1872 up to 1879, several states and railway companies began to default and investment fell. Capital returned to Europe or was diverted to Australia and India but the U.S. balance of payments recovered. In 1879 the import of capital was resumed and during the 1880s Europe is estimated to have contributed two-fifths of all the investment in U.S. railroads. From 1883 to 1890 over $1 billion was invested by Europe in the U.S.A. A crisis developed in 1890 due to the flooding of the U.S. market with railroad securities and a trade recession, and until 1896 there was a net disinvestment of European capital and a favourable U.S. balance of payments. From 1896 until World War I with only a slight pause at the turn of the century, another $1 billion flowed from Europe to the U.S.A. although this was not reflected in the U.S. balance of payments due to the start of a massive investment in Canada and Europe by the U.S.A.

2.5 SUMMARY

From the previous discussion and the various estimates arrived at it is possible to draw the following conclusions:

(1) The U.K. was by far the most important country involved in investment of all kinds in the U.S.A. Even by 1913, she still accounted for an amount approximately equal to all her other competitors put together.
(2) Direct investment in the U.S.A. from Europe prior to 1914 amounted to over $1.1 billion (1914 prices) — this figure excludes brewing and petroleum where important direct investments existed.
(3) Of the European countries involved, only the U.K. and Germany and to a much lesser extent France and Holland were significant.
(4) Direct investment of all kinds was at its pre-World War I maximum in 1913, when it represented a considerable proportion of total investment in the U.S.A.
(5) In considering the years 1870–1914 over 90 per cent of the total world foreign investment up to 1914 is automatically included.

3 The Historical Background to Foreign Investment in the U.S.A.

3.1 INTRODUCTION

The period 1865–1914 covers the 50 years from the end of the American Civil War to the start of World War I and in terms of direct investment in the U.S.A. was the most important in American history up to that time. This period is examined in Section 3.4. It is, however, important to consider the part played by European capital in the development of the U.S.A. before the Civil War and it is convenient to consider this in two parts. The first is the period from earliest colonial times to about 1800 and this is discussed in Section 3.2. The second period is that from about 1800 to the Civil War and this is discussed in Section 3.3. Section 3.5 explains the importance of the technological innovations of that time and explains why the country of origin often differed from that of development. Section 3.6 gives some data on the U.S. economy in 1914 and its growth up to that point. Finally, Section 3.7 looks at various attempts to estimate the numbers of companies actually involved in direct investment in manufacturing industry in the U.S.A. before 1914.

3.2 COLONIAL TIMES TO 1800

Before the 1800s almost all manufacturing in the U.S.A. was of the cottage industry type, although some industries were highly capitalised and relatively complex for the time, e.g. iron and shipbuilding. In a few instances industry was run by partnerships. There is evidence of only eight quasi-corporate entities in the whole of the U.S.A. prior to 1800.[1] These were all in either the textile or glass industries and ironically one was a German-owned glass works that was established in Fredericktown, Maryland, in 1789 but abandoned only a few years later.

Lewis states that in the early nineteenth century: 'the very diversity of these industries, the small size of most of the firms and the prevalence of the individual and partnership type of business organisation all served to discourage foreign participation in American enterprise'.[2] However, virtually all the initial capital required for early American colonisation was supplied by the U.K. and a great deal was taken physically to the U.S.A. by the emigrants themselves. This was required for the transport, early subsistence and defence of the colonists. There is no doubt that immigrant capital, speculative investments, long-term loans and trade credit financed by both private enterprise and the U.K. government laid the foundation of modern America and assured its development.[3] Prior to 1800 the four basic colonial industries were the iron, shipbuilding and tobacco industries and the naval stores trade. These relied almost entirely either directly or indirectly on British capital. So much so in fact, that by the time of the revolution against the British in 1775 the colonies were estimated to have accumulated debts to the U.K. of $40 million[4] although it is interesting to note that the U.K. Parliament, which was prepared to make awards to British people who had, as a result of the revolution, sustained losses in the U.S.A., only granted $15 million.

The problem of raising capital was not the only deterrent to investment in the U.S.A. in this early period — other critical shortages were skilled labour and power supplies. The latter meant that generally there were small mills on small streams with localised markets. The former is illustrated by the fact that Baron Stiegel, an entrepreneur 'who had poured money into his glassworks in Pennsylvania in the 1770s', was obliged to close it down because the skilled hands he had brought from Europe at great expense simply worked their passage and then departed to take advantage of free opportunities in the West.[5] Transportation difficulties compounded the problem.

Difficulties in the transfer of technology were also encountered; much technology was transferred verbally by immigrants.[6] Corporate forms do not seem to have been sufficiently developed to cope with the international transfer of complex technology. In addition, many countries, notably the U.K., passed laws in the eighteenth and early nineteenth centuries attempting to prohibit the outflow of technology.

There is virtually no evidence of capital other than from the U.K. involved in the U.S.A. at this time and the connections between the U.S.A. and the U.K., which dominated U.S. relations with Europe, would seem to justify this.

3.3 1800 TO THE CIVIL WAR

British capital made more impact on the U.S.A. in the first half of the nineteenth century than it had done previously. Despite the interruptions to commerce occasioned by the Napoleonic Wars in Europe and the Anglo-American War of 1812–15, by 1828 25 per cent of the entire U.S. national debt was held in the U.K. and within the next decade the majority of the vast U.S. cotton estates had been mortgaged to London merchants.[7] British capital at that time was chiefly in the form of state and corporation stocks and bonds but as time passed and opportunities widened, increasing portfolio capital found its way into the development of the vast U.S. transportation network, mainly the railways. Although other European countries as well as the U.K. were beginning to supply portfolio capital, the only country doing so to a significant degree was Holland. When expressed as a proportion of the total U.S. national wealth, the British and Dutch contribution never exceeded 10 per cent;[8] this was nonetheless a huge amount of capital and meant the difference between slow, self-generated development and the very rapid development which in fact occurred.

There was still only a negligible migration of corporate capital at that time and although the private U.K. investor avoided investing directly in a U.S. business venture, by investing in the multitude of stocks and bonds available, he was doing so indirectly. From 1820 onwards Baring Brothers (and other British finance houses) 'played the role of leading intermediary between the British capitalist and the American entrepreneur'.[9] The situation, however, was beginning to change. In 1862 the British Companies Act was passed and shortly afterwards it started to be imitated in the U.S.A. by laws which superseded the various state-conferred charters.[10] This act signalled the start of the limited liability company and meant that large-scale corporations were now feasible. It was not until the advent of these large corporations in the U.S.A. and the beginning of large-scale industry that followed, that foreign capital began to be drawn directly into U.S. manufacturing ventures.[11] One of the very few exceptions to this was the British control of the Mount Savage ironworks in 1844. This company was involved in manufacturing components for the railway industry. There were other small direct investments in rails, banking and insurance but as part of the overall flow of capital they were insignificant. In the U.S. domestic sector before 1860 a 'wide variety of manufacturing existed because of the isolation of the local market from imported goods as a result of high transfer costs'.[12]

Household manufacture declined as transport systems (e.g. the Erie canal) began to be expanded, and by 1860 had virtually disappeared.[13] Industry progressed from home and handicraft stages to a domestic stage, and finally the factory stage and foreign capital moved into canals, banks, railroads and merchandising trade.

The period before the Civil War saw the emergence of demands for a national economic policy as reflected in desire for the rapid creation of economic infrastructure (particularly public services and transport) and for common systems as exemplified by demands for the national regulation of banking and currency. This desire was, however, grafted on to a dual economy – the plantation economy of the South was not being developed by progress in the North. Consequently, in the 1840s protectionism was seen as a plank in creating a national community of interest. The tariff of 1842 provided an early stimulus for European investment in the protected economy. Further reasons were provided by the discovery of gold in California in 1848 and the subsequent 'gold rush' attracted both immigrants and capital to the new frontiers of the U.S.A. Against this, the default of several U.S. states retarded inflows of capital – U.S. credit reached its nadir in the early 1840s.

The general progress was halted, however, by severe depressions of 1819, 1837–44, 1857–8 (and the later 'crash' of 1873 which began with the collapse of Jay Cooke's banking enterprises, bringing down many other enterprises and leading to business stagnation, unemployment and collapsing farm prices). Even at the end of the period large enterprises existed only in the textiles industry of New England, in banking, importing and distribution, and of course, in the railroads. The early part of the period, to 1815, saw the heyday of the independent non-specialised urban merchant, through whom production was channelled to diffuse markets. British firms set up many such agents in New York, for example, and often used them for dumping excess inventories. However, the period 1815–70 saw the decline of such all-purpose merchants and they were replaced by specialised wholesalers. This change was necessitated by the increased complexity of products, the increasing concentration of markets (later to lead to the full internalisation of the distribution process by manufacturers) and the more direct transport system.[14]

3.4 THE CIVIL WAR TO WORLD WAR I

The period 1865—1914, which covers the 50 years from the American Civil War to World War I was unique in its suitability for the free movement of capital and technology on a worldwide basis. Dunning[15] has identified three reasons for this:

(1) The world at that time was sharply divided into capital exporting and capital importing countries whose needs and opportunities ideally complemented each other. Nations such as the U.S.A. and Australia were just at the take-off stage while other mature industrial nations, principally the U.K. and Germany, were, due to rapidly expanding national savings, in a position to supply the necessary capital.
(2) There were virtually no impediments to the migration of capital and people. With only a few exceptions, lending and borrowing countries actively encouraged the movement of these productive factors. McLain[16] argues that before and immediately after the Civil War, the migration of people, skills and enterprises contributed more to the growth of U.S. technology than did capital migration. Throughout the period the demand for British craftsmen and technicians was virtually insatiable.
(3) There were few foreign exchange problems and no transfer difficulties because of the rigid fixing of the world's currencies to gold. The international machinery, through which international investments were made, was more highly advanced and better equipped than its domestic counterpart. However, between 1863 and 1878 the dollar was not fixed to gold and the fluctuation of its value gave real problems for foreign investors, exporters and importers.[17]

As a result of these three factors the period from the end of the Civil War until the start of World War I saw, in addition to the established portfolio investment flow, the first really significant influx of foreign manufacturing concerns into the U.S.A. However, in spite of this swing from portfolio to direct investment evident during the period, a very large part of the flow of capital from Europe to the U.S.A. continued to be portfolio and railways continued to be the prime attraction. The importance of the railways and the part they played in the large-scale development of the American West cannot be emphasised enough. Edelstein[18] states that the principal supplier of U.S. assets to the U.K. capital market during the years 1870–1913 was the U.S. railway industry. U.S. Government securities were an important element in the U.S. component of U.K. portfolios at the beginning of the period but by 1880 U.S. railway securities were overwhelmingly the dominant element in the U.K. holdings of U.S. assets. He adds that it therefore seems reasonable to assume that conditions relating to U.S. railway investment and finance were the central determinants of the supply of U.S. assets offered in the U.K.

The period up to 1874 saw the end of dependence on the import of foreign manufactures. The Civil War encouraged large-scale organisations and innovations and it provided cheap money for entrepreneurs in the North.

Before and during the reconstruction era of the South (1865–77), two major contentions in U.S. economic policy were the level of the external tariff and the issue of paper money versus a gold-backed currency. It is rather too crude to see the first conflict as being simply Northern manufacturers versus Southern planters. Although some Northern industrialists fought for a high tariff (notably iron and steel manufacturers), the railroad and shipping interests preferred a low tariff, and wool manufacturers were protectionists provided that the duty on imported wool was not high (i.e. they wanted a high effective tariff on their manufacturing process). On the paper money issue, bondholders and most bankers wanted to return to gold but domestic manufacturers seeking capital wanted paper money combined with moderate inflation.[19]

In the U.S.A., three factors were particularly important in development. First and most important, the growth of the domestic market, fostered by inflows of immigrants; second, the decline in transport costs, the growth of urban centres and the establishment of distribution networks for imports and domestic manufacturers stimulated trade; third, the plentiful supplies of (high-quality) labour and entrepreneurial talent provided the basis for take-off.[20] The consequence of this final factor was the facility with which foreign innovations were adopted; indeed, a widespread and rapid development of mechanical skills took place. Proprietary knowledge was imported both legally and illegally from Europe and combined with a flexible and eager workforce. Specialisation and increase in the size of the firm was achieved because of the simultaneous development of several industries sharing similar technical processes. This was the basis on which American industrialisation was founded.

In addition, the U.S. government worked to build 'the minimum general system that enlarged personal opportunity' for the government realised that 'in creating markets, seeking efficiency, applying new technology and satisfying changing tastes, economic forces promoted national unity'.[21] 'Infant industry' policies were followed in an attempt to build up domestic industry behind tariff walls — as will be shown, this had the result of encouraging 'defensive investment' by foreign firms, to protect market positions built up initially by exports.

It is not difficult to see what a dynamic effect the flow of capital from the U.K. had on the development of the U.S.A.

A second factor distinguishing the period 1870—1914 was that by 1870 the flow of capital was no longer in only one direction. By that time, several large U.S. manufacturing enterprises were beginning to make direct investments in Europe and elsewhere.[22] Vernon states that towards the end of the nineteenth century while the U.S.A. was still importing large quantities of European capital, two or three dozen large firms had set up production units of appreciable size overseas, mainly in Canada and the U.K.[23] By the turn of the century he estimates that there were between 75 and 100 U.S.-controlled manufacturing plants operating outside the U.S.A.

A third factor that was unique to the period 1870—1914 was the cyclical nature of the flow of capital. While the cyclical pattern with regard to the U.S. balance of payments was discussed in Section 2.4, Morgan and Thomas[24] have examined its effects on the U.K. balance of payments. Even by 1914 when the U.K.'s share of the total inflow of capital to the U.S.A. had fallen to about 50 per cent, its lowest-ever point until then, it still represented a very large contribution and certainly large enough for any U.K. cyclicality to be reflected in the totals. Morgan and Thomas state that the U.K. balance of payments deteriorated sharply after 1872 and during the second half of the decade there was little if any surplus for overseas investment but the outward flow of capital resumed in the 1880s. They identify two further checks in the investment flow: one in 1890 after the Baring Bank crisis, and the second during the South African War when money was required to finance the war operation. The Baring Bank was saved from bankruptcy by a consortium of other institutions, but because it was one of the largest banks and also heavily involved in the U.S.A., the crisis was sufficient to reduce significantly the flow of U.K. capital to the U.S.A. at that time. The Baring crisis put a sudden stop to English syndicate capital movements.[25] In spite of these checks there was, as Morgan and Thomas point out, further phenomenal growth in U.K. investment in the U.S.A. between 1905 and 1914, and they estimated that between 1880 and 1914 the U.K. invested well over £2000 million worldwide of which a significant proportion went to the U.S.A. It has also been suggested that British outward investment was population-sensitive, which meant that capital and labour outflow from the U.K. were simultaneous. Court notes that 'the movement of capital is not intelligible without knowledge of the movement of people'.[26]

British efforts to gain control of U.S. industrial concerns seem to have reached their peak between 1885 and 1895 and much of the capital was subscribed by private investors in companies registered in the U.K. but operating in the U.S.A. After the crisis of 1873 when many American companies became bankrupt as a result of the U.S. trade recession, British investors began to feel that a greater measure of control was necessary[27] over the company being invested in. The type of syndicate investment described in Chapter 1 was found to be one method by which control could be achieved. The degree of control was inherently limited — individual members of syndicates were able to exercise very little control — but the syndicate as a whole, substantially more. The industries which were most popular with the syndicates (all of which are discussed in Chapter 4) were brewing and distilling, iron and steel and flour-milling. At some time syndicates invested in many other industries.

As time went on an increasing proportion of the portfolio capital flowing to the U.S.A. moved away from loan capital into equity holdings in industrial concerns and an increasing proportion of the total capital took the form of direct investment. Coram[28] suggests that by the first half of 1889 as much as $200 million had been invested in industrial concerns alone. As Dunning says: '... these were the years of vast speculative investments in cattle raising, mining, land and breweries. Projects that have long since been forgotten but which exerted a vital influence on U.S. economic development at that time.'[29] He estimates that by 1913, U.K. investment in the U.S.A. had reached an all-time peak of £755 million ($3650 million at the prevailing exchange rate). It is estimated that at the beginning of World War I one-tenth of British national income was earnings on investments abroad. Dunning gives the total foreign investment in the U.S.A. at that time as $7000 million, so although the U.K.'s contribution (as a percentage of the total) was falling, it was still over 50 per cent in 1913. It is difficult to estimate precisely the share of this British stake which was represented by corporate or direct investment but there is no doubt that, at that time, it far exceeded the value of corresponding American investment in the U.K.[30] What is important is that the period 1870–1914 saw the first ventures into the U.S.A. of what have become some of today's giant companies, such as Courtaulds, Lever Brothers, J. & P. Coats and English Sewing Cotton from the U.K. and Nestlé, Siemens, Solvay and Royal Dutch Shell from continental Europe. Dunning stresses the significant part played by U.S. subsidiaries of European companies, such as Royal Dutch Shell and Courtaulds, in the development of some of America's new industries.

The years 1895–1904 saw the first great merger and acquisition boom.[31] The merger boom was largely one of horizontal combination (companies joining at the same level of production). This boom saw the formation of many of today's American giant multinationals, amongst them U.S. Steel, Bethlehem Steel and Republic Steel, American Tobacco (now American brands), E. I. Dupont and General Electric. The close of this first merger boom was heralded by implementation of the Sherman Act (1890) and the emergence of U.S. Government anti-trust policies.

This policy resulted in three important legal decisions before World War I. In 1904, the Supreme Court held that a series of railroad mergers were illegal.[32] In 1911, action was taken against American Tobacco and Standard Oil Co. (N.J.).[33] The former forced American Tobacco to divest itself of R. J. Reynolds, Liggett & Meyers, P. Lorillard and United Cigar Stores, thus creating a competitive industry. The latter forced a *pro rata* distribution amongst shareholders of the assets of 33 companies acquired by Standard Oil from a pre-existing trust and instituted competition in this important industry. In 1914, section 7 of the Clayton Act (which was amended in 1950) gave teeth to the government's anti-merger drive. Despite this, 301 companies annually disappeared through merger during the period 1895–1904.[34] The period 1865–1914 saw the concentration of various industries into oligopolistic structures – notably in tobacco, petroleum, rubber, primary metals and electrical machinery, and the growth of national enterprises by backward integration, horizontal combination and the internalisation of distribution networks.

In the period immediately following the Civil War, railroads represented the only concentrated market for manufactured products. Railroads also pioneered the development of sophisticated management structures (bureaucratic control, centralised purchasing). However, market size and concentration increased and with the increasing complexity of technically based products, the need for control over raw material and intermediate goods input for economies of scale and for close and continuing contact between manufacturer and customer, led to integration backward, horizontally and into distribution.[35] This process led to fundamental reorganisation in production systems in large firms and in distribution, where in many industries it made wholesalers and jobbers redundant (although they continued to be important in standardised products with widely diffused markets).[36] The parallel development of the U.S. capital market – the Civil War gave a major stimulus to capital market development – and the willingness of banks and insurance companies to finance the building of giant companies, makes this period very important in the development of the modern U.S. economy. The two-fold thrust of concentration in markets and production, combined with advancing and increasingly complex technology, led to fully integrated production and distribution systems under the control of large national firms.

Although castigated as such, most of the large national firms formed at the turn of the century were not 'trusts'. Strictly a trust (as first developed by Standard Oil in 1882) is an exchange of trust certificates for the common stock of a group of corporations, thus avoiding the common law prohibition that one corporation shall not hold stock in another. This form of organisation declined after 1889 when New Jersey's corporate laws allowed a corporation chartered in that state to hold stock in others. Therefore virtually all corporations put together after 1889 were legally holding companies.

The latter part of the period 1870—1914 also saw a change in the corporate structure of European investment, towards the incorporation of subsidiaries in host countries rather than unincorporated branches. This meant a move towards greater autonomy of decision-making in the host country.[37]

The year 1914 was a landmark in the history of European investment in the U.S.A. Because of the war, which the U.S.A. entered in April 1917, the two largest investors were forced into totally different situations. All German-controlled subsidiaries in the U.S.A. were seized and the U.K. government was forced to liquidate about 70 per cent of the total U.K. investment in the U.S.A. to finance the war. This often had to be done at artificially low prices because of the prevailing unique circumstances, and although the investments were later partially rebuilt, the portfolio portion was never again to reach its pre-war level. Direct investment from the U.K., however, continued to increase, and by 1937 accounted for $833 million (£169 million approx.) out of the total U.K. overseas investment stake of £2743 million. Somewhat ironically Courtaulds' direct investment in the U.S.A., which was the most successful British venture there at the time, survived, to become the only British direct investment in the U.S.A. to be compulsorily sold during World War II. The British government then compelled the company to sell its 91 per cent interest in the American Viscose Corporation, at that time the largest man-made fibre concern in the world, for $54 million. This was only a fraction of the corporation's true market value and was totally against Courtaulds' wishes.

In terms of European investment in the U.S.A., the period 1870—1914 was unique in many ways and far more important than any previous one.

In terms of European direct investment in U.S. manufacturing industry, the period from 1870 to 1914 saw the start of the first significant investments, and as Vernon says, '... Looking back to that period it is interesting to note both the lateness and the suddenness with which Europe came to recognise the existence of the US as a potential industrial power'.[38] It was the delay in the U.S. industrial revolution, the risks caused by the Civil War and the upsurge in the rate of evolution after it, coupled with the fact that foreign direct investment in manufacturing at such a distance only became viable with new technology, which caused the lateness and suddenness.

3.5 THE IMPORTANCE OF INNOVATIONS AND THEIR ORIGINS

The period 1870–1914 was one of dramatic technological advance. As a general rule in the U.S.A., labour-saving innovations were the most successful. In spite of the vast migration of people to the U.S.A. there was a scarcity of labour for most of the period because of tremendous rates of development in the U.S. economy and the subsequent demand for both skilled and unskilled labour which immigration was unable to satisfy for most of the period.

The total abolition of slavery which coincided with the end of the Civil War in 1885, and which had started in the North nearly 100 years before, did not dramatically affect the employment situation. It simply required that the same labour was used as before, but on a different basis. In the cotton-growing industry it was Whitney's gin, invented in 1792, that had the most dramatic labour-saving consequences. Rather than causing a surplus of slave labour in the South, it enabled the existing workforce to vastly increase their output. In Europe the situation was different. There the scarcity was of raw materials, so innovations that could save raw materials were the most successful. The problem was not of labour shortage, but of unemployment. Nonetheless the majority of all innovations still came from Europe, although the U.S.A. was instrumental in the actual development and introduction of many of the products. One compilation, covering significant inventions from 1880 to 1899, shows that 63 per cent of them originated in Europe.[39]

Innovations in the textile and metal allied industries were mainly European in origin and, as discussed in Sections 4.3, 4.11 and 4.12, there were instances when complete industries moved from Europe to the U.S.A. Dunning mentions the pottery trade as another example.[40]

Franko has listed some of the continental European innovations and

TABLE 3.1 Some significant European inventions, 1864–1914

Invention	Firm	Country	Date	Stimulus
The ammonia soda process	Solvay	Belgium	1864	The high cost of fuel and sulphuric acid and the profit from the recovery of nitrogen-rich ammonia
Alizarin for dyestuffs	BASF	Germany	1870	The cut-off of the supply of natural dyes for military uniforms by the Franco-Prussian War
The synthesis of ammonia for fertiliser	BASF	Germany	1913	The scarcity of arable land, the intolerable strategic dependence on Chilean nitrates and the guaranteed military demand for explosives
The anti-syphilitic drugs (Salvarsin)	Hoechst	Germany	1910	Mass demand by low-income groups guaranteed by government health insurance
Margarine	Jurgens	Netherlands	1872	Mass demand by low-income groups due to the high price of butter

Source: L. G. Franko (1976), *The European Multinationals*, Harper & Row, p. 26.

the factors that stimulated their invention.[41] These are outlined in Table 3.1.

Solvay's ammonia soda process made the Leblanc process obsolete virtually overnight and enabled Solvay to start, through joint ventures, a series of direct foreign investments. The Leblanc industry survived because it generated several useful by-products which the Solvay process did not. Alizarin meant the start of the transition from natural to synthetic dyes and the supremacy of the German dye industry for many years. The synthesis of ammonia represented the first synthetic fertiliser and the reduction of European dependence on natural sources. Salvarsin meant a permanent cure for syphilis which at the time was very common; and margarine, although still dependent on natural products, represented a dramatic reduction in the price of a staple commodity and its availability to a wider market. These innovations are still relevant today, in some cases over 100 years after their invention. Many innovations were also successfully exploited by U.K. companies — an example is Courtaulds' very successful exploitation of the artificial silk process both in the U.K., and even more successfully, in the U.S.A. The transfer of capital without technological inputs was almost uniformly unsuccessful.

3.6 THE U.S. ECONOMY IN 1914

European direct investment contributed to the rapid development and industrialisation of the U.S.A. The net value of output in manufacturing did not overtake that of agriculture until the early 1880s and by that time the U.S.A. — with 29 per cent of the world's total manufacturing output — was the leading industrial nation.[42]

By 1914 the population of the U.S.A. had grown to 99,118,000 through natural growth and successive waves of immigration throughout the nineteenth century (see Table 3.2). Growth in real income was steady also (see Table 3.3), and the U.S.A. had become a high income and consumption economy. As Table 3.3 shows, income per capita in real terms trebled between the early 1870s and the end of World War I.[43]

These national aggregate income figures conceal an expanding manu-

TABLE 3.2 Population and immigration in the U.S.A., 1800—1920

Date	Estimated population (in 1000s as of 1 July)	Total immigration per year (decade average)
1800	5,297	n.a.
1810	7,224	n.a.
1820	9,618	12,850
1830	12,901	53,838
1840	17,120	142,734
1850	23,261	281,455
1860	31,513	208,126
1870	39,905	274,214
1880	50,262	524,857
1890	63,056	369,429
1900	76,094	820,238
1905	83,820	—
1910	92,407	634,738
1915	100,547	—
1920	106,466	—

Source: Calculated from *Historical Statistics of the United States.* U.S. Department of Commerce, Bureau of the Census 1960, p. 7 and pp. 56—7.

facturing sector which had grown from a 13.9 per cent contribution to national income in the 1870s to a 22.2 per cent share immediately before World War I. In the same period, the share of agriculture fell from 20.5 per cent to 15.2 per cent.[44] Clearly, this sectoral shift reflected changing direction for both domestic and foreign investment. The foreign inflow was clearly connected with the inflow of technology and with the changing industrial structure of the U.S.A., which is discussed in Chapter 4.

We should not underestimate the problem of communication within the U.S.A. and between the U.S.A. and Europe. New York was not linked to San Francisco by telegraph until 1861 and the same two cities were linked by telephone in 1915.[45] The Atlantic cable was laid in 1866. These communication barriers presented significant problems for national and particularly international control of investments.

3.7 PREVIOUS INVESTIGATIONS OF EUROPEAN DIRECT INVESTMENTS

Previous investigations of European direct investment in the U.S.A. before World War I, by Franko[46] of continental European investors and

TABLE 3.3 Total and per capita G.N.P. of the U.S.A., 1869–1921, in current and constant (1929) prices

5-year annual average	Current prices		1929 constant prices		Implicit price index (1929 = 100)
	Total $ (billion)	Per capita ($)	Total $ (billion)	Per capita ($)	
1869–1873	6.7	165	9.1	223	74
1872–1867	7.5	171	11.2	254	67
1877–1881	9.2	186	16.1	327	57
1882–1886	11.3	204	20.7	374	55
1887–1891	12.3	199	24.0	388	51
1889–1893*	13.1	204	26.1	405	50
1889–1893	13.5	210	27.3	424	49
1892–1896	13.6	199	29.6	434	46
1897–1901	17.3	231	37.1	496	47
1902–1906	24.2	294	46.8	569	52
1907–1911	31.6	349	55.0	608	57
1912–1916	40.3	408	62.5	632	64
1917–1921	75.9	719	71.9	683	105

* This figure and those before, calculated according to Kuznet's concept of G.N.P. – those after calculated according to Department of Commerce concept of G.N.P.
Source: As Table 3.2, p. 139.

34   *European Direct Investment in the U.S.A. before World War I*

by Stopford[47] of U.K. investors, have been exercises in 'projecting backwards' from the multinational companies of today. Consequently, they do not attempt to be exhaustive studies of all such investment. Obviously, many investments were made by European companies which are no longer in existence and there are cases where investments have become locally owned.

Table 3.4 is Franko's list of current continental European multinational companies which had U.S. subsidiaries before 1913. They can be accounted for as follows: Fiat of Italy jointly owned a car assembly plant near New York, Solvay of Belgium had a holding in the Solvay Process Company, Geigy and Nestlé of Switzerland both had U.S. subsidiaries and the latter was to merge with the Anglo-Swiss Condensed Milk Company, whose several U.S. subsidiaries had been sold to the (U.S.) Borden Company in 1902 (see Chapter 5). Germany was represented by Siemens, Degussa, Bosch, Bayer, Metallgesellschaft and Daimler Benz. Degussa is the only

TABLE 3.4   Number of continental European parent systems with U.S. subsidiaries in 1913 by country

Country	Number of parents	Number of subsidiaries
Germany	6	7
Netherlands	2	2
France	1	1
Belgium and Luxembourg	1	1
Switzerland	2	2
Italy	1	1
TOTAL	13	14

Source: Franko (1976), p. 163.

firm in Franko's list which had more than one subsidiary, for it operated the Niagara Electrochemical Company and Roessler and Hasslacher. This accounts for the total seven subsidiaries of German firms in Table 3.4. The Dutch companies are presumably Margarine Uni and Royal Dutch Shell. The French subsidiary to which Franko refers is presumably Michelin. Lewis also mentions the New York Taxi Cab Co. Ltd, in which the French stake amounted to $1.683 million in 1914, and the Berlitz chain of language schools as companies with significant French interest.[48] Interestingly, Péchiney's plans for an aluminium smelter in the U.S.A. were aborted by the outbreak of war.

In a different exercise, Franko has identified the locations of other foreign subsidiaries of firms with U.S. investments.[49] These are shown in Table 3.5. The list includes S.K.F. of Sweden who did not start production in the U.S.A. until after the war had begun in Europe. Franko makes the point that, despite the flood of American companies investing in Europe after World War II, continental European multinationals began to emerge at the same time as U.S. ones, and that before World War I they were just as prolific. All German-owned subsidiaries still operating at the start of the war were seized by the Alien Property Custodian and attempts were made to dispose of these assets to American interests.

TABLE 3.5 Location of foreign manufacturing of selected continental European companies about 1914

Parent firm and country	Industry	Locations
Switzerland		
Geigy	Chemicals	U.S.A., Russia, France, Germany, U.K., Austria
Nestlé	Food	U.S.A., Germany, U.K., Spain, Holland, Norway, Australia
Germany		
Siemens	Electrical	U.S.A.(f), Russia, France(f), U.K., Spain, Austria
Degussa	Chemicals	U.S.A., Spain, Belgium
Bosch	Electrical	U.S.A., France, U.K., Japan
Bayer	Chemicals	U.S.A., Russia, France
Metallgesellschaft	Non-ferrous metals	U.S.A., France(f), U.K., Austria, Holland, Belgium
Daimler Benz	Automobiles	U.S.A., U.K., Austria
Netherlands		
Margarine Uni	Food	U.S.A.(w), Germany, U.K.
Belgium		
Solvay	Chemicals	U.S.A., Russia, France, Germany, U.K., Spain, Austria, Italy
Sweden		
S.K.F.	Machinery	U.S.A.(w), Russia(w), France, Germany, U.K.

Notes: (f) = failed or abandoned before World War I.
(w) = entered between the years 1914 and 1918.

Source: Franko (1976), p. 9.

36 *European Direct Investment in the U.S.A. before World War I*

TABLE 3.6   U.K. companies with U.S. manufacturing subsidiaries before 1914

Company		Product
Original title	*Current title*	
J. & P. Coats	Coats Paton	Cotton thread
English Sewing Cotton	Tootal	Cotton thread
Courtaulds	Courtaulds	Synthetic textiles
Lever Brothers	Unilever	Soap
Reckitt and Sons	Reckitt and Colman	Starch
Royal Dutch Shell	Royal Dutch Shell	Petroleum products

Source: Stopford (1974), pp. 316–17.

In a similar exercise, Stopford lists six U.K. companies which had manufacturing operations in the U.S.A. before 1914. These are detailed in Table 3.6.

Reckitt and Sons was established in 1840 in Hull, England to manufacture starch.[50] Reckitt's opened a New York branch in 1892. Through a mutual contact, Reckitt's became acquainted with the American firm, Morse Brothers, and in 1896 purchased the British Empire rights to Morse Brothers' 'Rising Sun' stove polish and 'Sun' paste stove polish.

In 1903 Reckitt's decided to enter the U.S. market directly — if possible by buying the Morse business (and Prescott's, with whom they had earlier had negotiations for 'Enamaline' grate polish when Reckitt's obtained the U.K. rights). Investigations began in 1904, when three of the Reckitt family went to the U.S.A. Although no terms could be agreed with Prescott's an agreement was signed with the Morse firm. However, Reckitt's directors were kept waiting months for final completion. The deal fell through. Morse Brothers had to pay 'a substantial sum' for breaking the agreement, and Reckitt's failed to become deeply involved in the U.S. grate polish market. However, Reckitt's bought a factory in New Brunswick for the manufacture of Blue and a separate company; Reckitt's (U.S.A.) Ltd, was formed in 1908. The factory was closed following the 1926 purchase of R.T. French Company of Rochester (N.Y.) by Colman's, with whom Reckitt's had begun pooling overseas companies. This pooling led eventually to merger in 1938. The production of the New Brunswick factory was transferred to the new Rochester plant, when French's, Reckitt's and Colman's U.S. production was rationalised under the umbrella of a new U.S. sales company, the Atlantis Sales Corporation. The other firms in the list are dealt with in the next two chapters.

TABLE 3.7 U.K. companies with 'outpost' manufacturing facilities in the U.S.A. before 1914

Company		Product
Original title	Current title	
Albright & Wilson	Albright & Wilson	Chemicals
Greens of Wakefield	E. Green & Son Limited	Engineering
Howard & Bullock	Stone Platt Industries	Textile machinery
Mackintosh	Rowntree Mackintosh	Foodstuffs
United Alkali	I.C.I.	Chemicals

Source: Stopford (1974), p. 324.

Stopford also mentions five other U.K. companies which he describes as having merely 'outpost' manufacturing facilities. This implies that the actual investment in production was very limited. These are listed in Table 3.7. E. Green & Son Limited of Wakefield[51] is one firm listed by Stopford which had an 'outpost' manufacturing facility. The firm was founded in 1821 in Wakefield, Yorkshire, by Edward Green and was incorporated as a limited liability company in 1888. In May 1892, only 4 years after incorporation, the Fuel Economizer Company of Matteawan was incorporated with Frank Green, grandson of the founder, as first president. The company's main product was a fuel economiser which recycled the residual heat of air or gases from (steam) boilers.

In 1902, the American business of the company 'showed a tendency to decline owing to the imposition of tariffs on economisers sent to the United States'. A visit from a manager of the U.S. company to Wakefield persuaded the firm to reorganise its American affiliate more effectively to meet the challenge of tariffs. The company's title was changed to the Green Fuel Economizer Company of Matteawan. The works of the new company were established at Beacon and the business flourished during the heyday of the cast iron vertical economiser. Green's made George Usher, who had previously been the firm's sales representative in Germany, first the sales manager, then the general manager of the U.S. firm. Usher wanted the firm to enter the field of combustion engineering and specifically to begin to market fans, but this was opposed by the parent company so Usher left the firm. This decision shows that control was firmly with the parent company. However, when a fan-making company started to compete in the economiser field, Green's decided to reverse this policy and to manufacture fans, which became a staple output of the U.S. firm.

After John Mackintosh, the founder of the toffee company in Halifax, Yorkshire, achieved national distribution throughout Britain he began to seek worldwide market coverage. In 1903 he began preparations for production in the U.S.A., followed by the establishment of a factory at Crefeld, near Cologne in Germany in 1906, and then in Canada and Australia.

Mackintosh's involvement with the U.S.A. began in 1903 when, accompanied by his brother-in-law, he made a 'lightning tour' of the U.S.A. and Canada.[53] High levels of duty on the import of confectionery provided the main motive for manufacture in the U.S.A. A factory at Astbury Park, on the Atlantic seaboard in New Jersey, was purchased and production began in 1904, backed by a large advertising effort (£100,000 over two years with the infant J. Walter Thompson company). The factory was staffed partly by workers brought from the English works. Market research, however, had not been undertaken, and although the toffee (sold in large slabs and broken by hammer at point-of-sale) sold well in winter, it melted in summer and proved unsaleable. The long distances also placed a heavy burden on distribution. The U.S. venture proved a failure and 'after three or four years' it was closed.[54] This failure cancelled all the profits made in the U.K. and for a time severely tested the survival of the whole firm.

Later ventures in the U.S.A., resumed in 1922, were at Viscount Mackintosh's (the founder's son) insistence, and were always joint ventures. The product was also more carefully presented, wrapped and packaged.

The lists of firms given by Franko and Stopford do not include companies controlling U.S. subsidiaries which failed or those which are not part of today's European multinationals. Lewis listed industrial companies operating direct investments before World War I but admitted the list was incomplete.[55] Table 3.8 shows that among British pre-war investments was the Marconi Wireless Telegraph Co. of America, formed in 1899, only

TABLE 3.8 European companies operating direct investments in the U.S.A. pre-World War I

Foreign company	Year of establishment	Notes
1. British-controlled		
(a) Courtaulds	1909	Initial capital $1.6 million. Reincorporated 1915 as Viscose Co. with all $9,999,500 issued capital stock held by parent
(b) Dunlop Pneumatic Tyre Co. Ltd	Established pre-1919 Reincorporated 1919	Reincorporated 1919 as Dunlop Tyre and Rubber Corporation of America — by 1923 fixed assets valued at $16 million

Foreign company	Year of establishment	Notes
(c) Glasgow and Western Exploration Company	?	Liquidated during World War I. Approximately $5 million expended in development of the mines and smelters in 15 years preceding the War
(d) Kelly's Directories Ltd	1890	Original capital investment $100,000
(e) Linen Thread Co.	–	Formed 1898 primarily as international holding company; by 1915 acquired all outstanding capital stock of five concerns operating mainly in U.S.A.
(f) Marconi's Wireless Telegraph Co. Ltd	?	Progressively expanding American business subsequent to 1914 through U.S. subsidiary Marconi Wireless Telegraph Co. of America
(g) Morell & Co.	?	English packing concern with two plants in Iowa ante-dating the War
(h) Williams Harvey & Co. Ltd	?	Held one-third interest in Williams Harvey Corporation
(i) The Sterling Trust Ltd	?	Wholly owned Railroads Lands Co. Ltd
(j) Fine Spinner and Doublers Association	?	Wholly owned Delta & Pine Land Company of Mississippi (Scott, Mississippi)
(k) Rolls-Royce Ltd	1919	Control held by parent company through ownership of all no-par common stock, while capital was supplied by Americans through $3.5 m preferred stock issue
(l) Bradford Dyers' Association	1911	$1 m dyeing plant established in Niantic, Washington County, New York including takeover of existing plant
(m) Claudius Ash, Sons & Co. Ltd	?	–
(n) Forestal Land, Timber & Railways Co. Ltd	?	–
(o) J. & P. Coats	1870	–
(p) Raphael Tuck & Sons Ltd	?	–
(q) U.S. Trust Corporation	?	–
2. *Belgian-controlled*		
(a) Belgium-Bohemian Mining Co.	?	–
(b) Jualin Alaska Mine	?	– Showed good results particularly (b)
3. *French-controlled*		
Andre Michelin et Cie	?	–

Source: Lewis (1936), pp. 570–2 and author's research.

2 years after the British parent company (see Figure 3.1). From 1899 until the formation of the Radio Corporation of America in 1919, Marconi companies were the dominant concerns in British and American wireless.[5 6] Despite its commanding position, Marconi's early years were unsuccessful in the investor's terms, for British Marconi did not pay dividends between 1897 and 1910. This position of dominance was reinforced by the fact that British stations all over the world refused to communicate with ships having equipment other than Marconi. In addition, the principal early American rival of Marconi, United Wireless, went into bankruptcy in 1912 (a contributing factor was that the company was found guilty of infringing Marconi patents), and its assets were acquired by British and American Marconi. Between 1912 and 1917 over 90 per cent of U.S. ship-to-shore radio communication was carried out by Marconi. Figure 3.1 shows the principal Marconi enterprises worldwide, established between 1897 and 1917.

Figure 3.1 Principal Marconi Interprises, 1897–1917

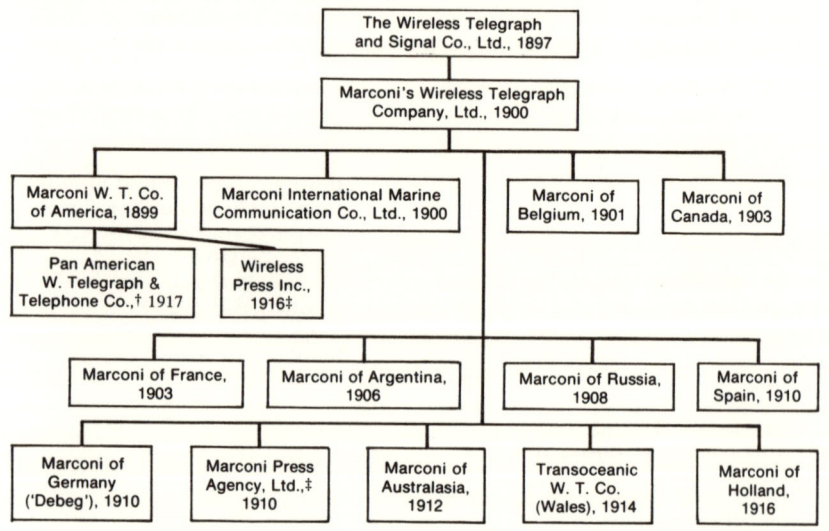

*In a number of foreign subsidiaries, the full titles are not given.

†This was organised jointly by British Marconi, American Marconi, and Federal Telegraph, to develop radio communication in South America.

‡These subsidiaries operated a general printing and publishing business for wireless books and periodicals.

Source: W. Rupert MacLaurin (1949), *Invention and Innovation in the Radio Industry*, Macmillan, p. 43.

The early development of the Marconi companies is marked by wrangles with governments and by British government protection, as radio communications were becoming a 'lifeline of Empire'. The founder, Guglielmo Marconi, of wealthy Irish–Italian ancestry, had difficulty in establishing 'smooth business relations'[57] and was rather obsessed with the technical side of the business. A major weakness of the company was its attention to perfecting existing models rather than reaching out for radically new discoveries in wireless — a focus on 'next year's model'.

During the war, the U.S. subsidiary of Marconi erected a very powerful up-to-date transmitting station at New Brunswick and built an important radio manufacturing plant at Aldene, New Jersey. However, during and after World War I pressure began to be felt for American control of such a vital strategic industry. (In 1905 Telefunken Corporation of Germany also had established a subsidiary in New York with a powerful station. In addition, this company manufactured and sold transmitting and receiving apparatus of high quality.[58]) F. D. Roosevelt and U.S. Navy officials (the Acting Secretary of the Navy, and later, the Assistant Secretary) were strongly in favour of establishing a U.S.-controlled international communications company. In 1919 the U.S. shipping board refused to allow American Marconi to equip shipping board vessels unless the company could furnish an affidavit showing that over 50 per cent of the stock was owned by U.S. citizens, which Marconi could not do. In 1919 the General Electric Company purchased a controlling interest in American Marconi and in 1920 the Radio Corporation of America was formed, when the assets of American Marconi were transferred to R.C.A.

It is perhaps surprising, to modern thinking, that such an important strategic firm stayed out of domestic hands for so long, especially as this included a period of world war. However, the most important firms were organised around one important inventor and initially at least, the commercial potentialities of wireless seemed remote. The Marconi company also shows a significant internal development from inventor/entrepreneur/owner domination to a more rounded form of organisation, almost joint control between a technical expert and a businessman (Godfrey Isaacs) brought into control business policy.

The majority of the companies in Table 3.8 are discussed at greater length in the analysis by industry in Chapters 4 and 5. It is clear, however, that many other companies, now defunct and forgotten, also crossed the Atlantic by direct investment before the outbreak of World War I. The history of their failure is just as interesting as the success which led to a nascent multinationalism in the surviving companies.

3.8 SUMMARY

The U.S.A. had an important input of foreign capital from the period of its colonisation right up to World War I. Earlier portfolio injections and cottage-type industry transfers were gradually replaced by investments approximating to 'modern' direct investment. The period from the end of the Civil War to World War I was particularly important in America's transition to industrialisation. Dependence on imported manufactures ended, large-scale industrial organisations grew, a national market began to emerge and innovations in products and processes fuelled the modernisation.

Foreign investment played a major role in these processes. The package of direct investment provided capital, skills, technology and know-how from Europe. As we shall see, this was not evenly diffused across industries but concentrated in a few areas where European advantages were greatest and most easily transferrable, given the cost and difficulties of communication and control.

By 1914 the U.S.A. had become the leading industrial nation. Its population of nearly 100 million was growing and disposable income growth accelerating. With these changes came changes in the nature and orientation of inward foreign investment. These changes are traced by industrial sector in the chapter which follows and individual investments are investigated in detail in Chapter 5.

4 A Review by Industry of the Areas where Direct Investment Occurred 1870–1917

4.1 INTRODUCTION

It is possible to identify several U.S. industries that were particularly suited to foreign direct investors and these are discussed individually in Sections 4.2–4.16. Section 4.15, which deals with the railway industry, is included not because it was the location of very much direct investment, but because of its unique importance. Although overall investment in the railway industry dwarfed all other areas of investment, relatively little direct investment in railroads took place, as will be seen in Section 4.15. In these industry sections as many companies as possible are named in order to give an idea of the numbers involved.

In the majority of the earliest examples (i.e. pre-1860) very little information about the exact nature of the investment is known and in some cases it is doubtful if they would in fact conform to the modern concept of direct investment. Comparatively few are subsidiaries of European manufacturers but were either new companies formed in Europe to operate in the U.S.A., or existing U.S. companies where some or all of the stock had been bought by European interests. Section 4.17 deals with various other industries where only isolated cases of direct investment took place. These include the U.S. soap industry, where although only one European company (Lever Brothers) made a direct investment, this investment was to become one of the largest of those in any industry.

4.2 THE CHEMICAL AND DYESTUFFS INDUSTRIES

A notable feature of the U.S. chemical industry before 1914 was the virtual absence of a dyestuffs sector which was already well established in Germany and Switzerland.[1] Synthetic dyes were invented in Germany and the German industry, maintained by cartels, was very strong. This successfully prevented other European countries as well as the U.S.A. from starting their own manufacturing operations. In the early 1870s the Germans first became active in the U.S. market, mainly through the use of exports rather than overseas production facilities.

Until about 1885 the German, and to a lesser extent the Swiss, companies used local export firms to service the underdeveloped countries of the world excluding the U.S.A. Sales in both Europe and the underdeveloped countries were handled by local wholesalers or agents, or both, who usually represented only one dyestuff manufacturer. After 1885, however, the manufacturers began to take over the wholesaling of their own products. As the contracts with the various marketing and wholesaling firms expired, they were not renewed and instead, trained salesmen and travelling consultants were sent to open sales offices in the major world commercial centres. These were often 'dummy' sales companies whose huge annual turnovers were out of all proportion to their tiny capital.[2] They were usually headed by Germans but used local people as technical consultants and salesmen where possible.

Prior to the early 1870s, the American firm of Thomas Holliday in Brooklyn, Boston and Philadelphia had the U.S. market to itself but at that time one of the first German entrants, Gustav Siegle, opened a New York office to handle sales of aniline dyes.[3] Siegle became the agent for Badische (BASF), although this was later transferred to the U.S. firm of Kuttroff, Pickhardt & Co. In 1882, the German firm of Bayer helped found the Hudson River Aniline Works but in 1883 the duty on imported dyes was considerably lowered and over the next few years five out of the original nine indigenous dyestuff manufacturers went out of business. Apart from Schoellkopf Aniline and Chemical Works of Buffalo which by 1914 controlled 10 per cent of the U.S. dyestuffs market, the market was controlled by the Germans and Swiss, mainly in the form of exports to the U.S.A., and even Schoellkopf had to import 90 per cent of raw materials.

Germany's development of the artificial dyestuffs originated when the Napoleonic continental blockade of the early nineteenth century prevented access to her traditional sources of raw material for natural dyes.[4]

The Swiss industry, which was largely based on copying the Germans to satisfy its own textile industry, had developed in parallel.

According to Tugendhat,[5] Friedrich Bayer had previously taken a share in an aniline plant at Albany, New York State in 1865 as well as the 1882 Hudson River works — this only 2 years after establishing his chemical company near Cologne. He had discovered that it would be cheaper to manufacture near the consumer than to do so in Germany and pay the shipping costs to the U.S.A. Geigy, the Swiss firm, which had been represented by an agency in New York since the 1870s, developed this into a manufacturing plant in 1903,[6] although it is not clear on what scale this operated.

According to McClain,[7] Bayer was the only German dyestuff firm with substantial manufacturing facilities in the U.S.A. prior to 1914. The Bayer factory at Rensselaer, New York, produced only a limited number of dyestuffs and pharmaceuticals including aspirin. These were later sold to the Sterling Drug Co., which had been taken over by the American government during World War I. In fact, the Sterling Drug Co. continued to market its predecessor's aspirin under the name Bayer Aspirin,[8] after the war. Bayer had originally been forced to manufacture in the U.S.A. for two reasons:

(1) very high tariffs were imposed on drug imports into the U.S.A. (often up to 100 per cent), which made it difficult for the company to compete;
(2) the patents on its drug Phenacetin (a forerunner of aspirin) had expired.

Friedrich Bayer's son and another German chemist Duisberg were later to spend many weeks in the U.S.A. studying the newly formed American Trusts. They looked closely at United States Steel and Standard Oil and their claims to have effected improvements in the fields of finance, manufacture and distribution. Duisberg was impressed with what he saw and became instrumental in the then unsuccessful attempt to form a German dye industry trust. Although this failed, many more mergers and cartels followed including the celebrated (or infamous) I.G. Farben trust, formed in 1925 when Bayer merged with Hoechst and BASF after an 'informal arrangement' dating from 1916. In 1908 the Bayer Company was involved in no less than 25 cartel agreements, which shows the extent to which the cartel system was being used.

The German dyestuffs companies, operating in such a totally different framework of law and opinion to that existing in the U.K. and U.S.A., steadily amalgamated with each other, cutting out competition at home in order to turn their united strength to the conquest of overseas markets.⁹ In the 10 years before 1914, there were only two groups of any consequence in the German industry and between them competition was regulated. It has been estimated that in 1914 the Germans controlled 88 per cent of the world's trade in dyestuffs with virtually no direct investment in overseas manufacture. The presence of cartels in many industries and nations prevented much foreign direct investment in the U.S.A. in favour of licensing or exporting from Germany, even as an evolution from exporting, and this was particularly true in the dye industry.¹⁰ It also contributed to the lack of German investment in the U.S. dye industry which may have seemed strange when their control of the U.S. market is considered.

In the chemical industry, the U.S.A. was not involved in the dramatic changes that occurred as a result of the discovery of the Solvay process. Previously, all production of soda, a vital raw material of many other industries including soap production, had been on the Leblanc system. This became obsolete virtually overnight and many Leblanc system producers who could not change over went out of business; others survived because of the valuable by-products of Leblanc which the new process did not produce, while many new companies based on the Solvay process were later established. The U.S.A. did not have this problem until the mid-1880s. It was entirely dependent on imports from the U.K. for all its alkali needs because the U.S.A. had no indigenous manufacturing plants. However, over the next 15–20 years its own alkali industry grew up behind a tariff wall designed to safeguard it from foreign competition. Between the 1890 McKinley and 1897 Dingley tariffs the duty on soda ash went up from £1.15 to £1.72 per ton and bleaching powder, once duty free, was subjected to a levy of £0.9 per ton.¹¹ Four companies, including the Solvay Process Company (see Chapter 5) with factories at Syracuse and Detroit, were operating within this protection and their output of 150,000 tons of ammonium soda in 1895 rose to 350,000 tons in 1900.

The Solvay Process Corporation was incorporated in 1881 and operational in 1884.¹² It was the idea of William B. Cogswell who persuaded the Solvay brothers in Belgium to grant him a licence. They put up one-third of the money for a plant, and Cogswell and some Syracuse businessmen found the rest. Solvay & Cie also supplied all the drawings and trained some of the technical staff at Dombusle in Belgium.

Other European chemical firms were also involved in the U.S.A. In 1898 the Albright and Wilson company were operating a subsidiary in the Niagara Falls area called the Oldbury Electrochemical Company. There the company produced white phosphorus for the match trade, which at that time was subject to a high import duty; chlorates were also produced, and the company leased the site and obtained its power from the Niagara Falls Power Company.[13] A competitor was a subsidiary of the United Alkali Company of the U.K. This was another electrochemical firm, the North American Chemical Company of Bay City, Michigan, and it began to produce potassium chlorate there in 1898.[14]

The German company, Deutsche Gold und Silber Scheideanstalt (usually known as Degussa) was established in 1868, and owned an American subsidiary, the Niagara Electrochemical Company, which was founded jointly with the Aluminium Co. Ltd in 1895 to make sodium and sodium cyanide. Also involved in Niagara was another U.S. subsidiary of Degussa, Roessler and Hasslacher, which produced cyanides.[15]

The Alien Property Custodian mentions other German chemical or dyestuff companies that were active in the U.S.A. around 1917 although mainly in a very small way. These were firms such as Badishe, Berlin, Hoechst, Cassella, Kalle and Hayden.[16] Some of the lesser-known firms must have been pretty obscure and the subsidiaries of the better-known firms very small.

In pharmaceuticals at least two American subsidiary companies, Merck and Schering, were offshoots of German parents towards the end of the 1800s. In 1927 Merck absorbed Rosengarten and Sons which had been founded in 1822 by a German–Swiss company, and was amalgamated with a U.S. company in 1905.[17] In general chemicals the General Aniline and Film Company (G.A.F.), although now American, was formerly part of an I.G. Farben subsidiary.

There were therefore many instances of foreign direct investment but most appear to have been short-lived. The largest and most successful was, without doubt, the Solvay Process Corporation. European research, though, was vital to the establishment and development of the U.S. chemical and pharmaceutical industries.

4.3 THE TEXTILE INDUSTRY

One of the first U.S. ventures by a European company was in 1865 when William Barbour & Sons of Lisburn, Northern Ireland, established the Barbour Flax Company at Paterson, New Jersey. The Barbour Group, with headquarters at New York and a second factory in Allentown, Pennsylvania, later became the largest flax thread manufacturer in the U.S.A.[18] Several other U.K. companies set up in the U.S.A. about that time. W. & J.

Knox of Kilburnie, Scotland, set up a similar plant in Baltimore and in 1881 Finlayson Bousfield & Co., also of Scotland, opened a yarn and thread factory at Grafton, Massachusetts. In common with Barbour, and indeed with the lace industry, they brought many of their own workers with them. A third Scottish company, Marshall and Company, opened a plant in New Jersey also around that time, making thread for the neighbouring boot and shoe industry. In 1898 these companies and some others under the direction of the parent Barbour Company in Ireland combined to form the Linen Thread Company with a capital of £2 million.[19] This move was instigated by competition and a general move towards rationalisation in the industry. In 1906 the new company took over the Boston Thread and Twine Company and for over 50 years two-thirds of the U.S. linen thread production was controlled by the U.K. until 1959, when Barbour sold its U.S. interests to the Indian Thread Mills Company.

In the cotton thread industry J. & P. Coats, the Glasgow company, sold about 75 per cent of its production in the U.S.A. until the Civil War, but new tariffs led the company to set up a factory at Pawtucket, Rhode Island in 1869. Coats purchased a twisting mill which had been constructed the year before on a small plot of land 100 feet square by the Conant Thread Company. This venture was highly successful and by 1890 was bigger than the parent company's mills in Paisley. In that year the Kerr and Clark Thread Co. (established in Paisley in 1851 by a George A. Clark and his brother-in-law) moved to Fall River, Massachusetts, in the U.S.A. and soon after it was bought by Coats. In 1864, the J. & J. Clark Company from Paisley set up a factory at Newark, New Jersey after a period from 1856 when George A. Clark was sole agent for both Clark and Kerr's. In 1883 the Clark Mile-end Company set up its first mills in New Jersey to twist and spool imported U.K. thread. In 1896 Coats bought out the Clark companies as well as several other U.K. firms and according to Plummer then owned 16 factories in the U.K. and U.S.A.[20] Coats & Clark Inc., the American subsidiary, then controlled between one-third and one-half of all the U.S. cotton thread production.[21] In the U.K. at that time, the English Sewing Cotton Co. Ltd, an amalgamation of a number of English manufacturers in 1897, was formed. Inspired by this move, 14 U.S. thread producers merged in 1898 with a capital of $18 million. In 1901 the combination controlled two-thirds of the U.S. production of cotton thread. English Sewing Cotton took 720,000 of the 1.2 million £5 ordinary shares and J. & P. Coats bought £100,000 of preference shares.[22] The new company was called the American Thread Company and since then Coats & Clark and the American Thread Company have controlled four-fifths of the U.S. cotton thread industry. The potential profitability of the U.S. investment is shown by the fact that the American Thread Company, in the first 17 years of its life (1899–1916), paid 12 annual dividends varying from 10 to 18 per cent and in only 2 years did it fail to pay anything.[23]

Coats & Clark Inc. have gone from strength to strength in the U.S.A. and are still, at least nominally, controlled from the U.K. In 1907, *The Economist* said of the Coats company:

> As it is the foremost of industrial companies in the country, so it is one of the best managed. The policy of the directors has always been conservative in the extreme, in the way of building up large reserves against all possible contingencies, and in keeping machinery and so forth thoroughly efficient and well up to modern requirements.[24]

There lie several indications of early success in foreign direct investment. The Pawtucket mill grew from 100 feet square to a site of 55 acres, but was closed in 1965 (the Newark plant ended manufacturing in 1948) and manufacturing, in common with much of the textile industry, has moved to the South. Coats & Clark operations now cover the East Coast of the U.S.A. from North to South and thread remains the central product, although considerable diversification has taken place.[25]

The only other notable U.K. textile venture in the U.S.A. was that of Courtaulds (see Chapter 5). In 1908, Courtaulds set up an American sales agency to sell rayon, and 2 years later to exploit the American patents acquired from the General Artificial Silk Co. (later Genasco Silk Works). Manufacturing began at a new plant at Marcus Hook, Pennsylvania, in 1910. By 1911 600 people were employed and within another year $1 million of extensions were being built and Courtaulds were financing the building of 66 houses locally for their employees.[26] In 1915, after several recapitalisation schemes, the company was reorganised into the Viscose Corporation employing 2500 people, and Courtaulds' investment was by then $15 million. The company was compulsorily taken over by American interests during World War II.

A few other investments in the textile industry also took place before 1914. J. & J. Cash began to manufacture their woven name tapes in Connecticut in 1906 because demand from the U.S.A. had become too great for their U.K. operation to satisfy. The Bradford Dyers' Association opened a textile commission finishing plant at Westerly, Rhode Island, in 1911, which it still owns. Titus Salt produced velvet plush and pile fabrics at Bridgeport, Rhode Island, in the 1880s, but this factory was absorbed by American interests in 1893. In the woollen trade, Forstmann and

Huffmann, which began to export cloth from Germany to the U.S.A. in 1853, were 'impelled by the high duties recently imposed by the Dingley tariff' to erect a mill in Passiac, New Jersey, in 1903. This involved 'bringing over nearly a full complement of machinery and probably a number of technicians and foremen, and setting up ... [in the U.S.A.] ... as near a replica as possible of the German establishment'. Between the wars, Forstmann and Huffmann became established as a leading manufacturer of dress goods in the U.S.A. Cole concludes that foreign investment in the woollen industry was of distinct value to the U.S.A. and that it stimulated appreciably the advance of domestic production.[27] Finally, the well-known American firm, Botany, was one of the many German-controlled firms taken over and sold by the Alien Property Custodian during World War I. The Germans had controlled Botany since 1890, when Botany Worsted Mills were established in Passiac, New Jersey, by Kammgarnspinnere, Stoehrond Co., AG which supplied capital and know-how.[28]

The instances of direct investment in U.S. textiles are, as in the chemical industry, dwarfed by two particular examples. In textiles these were the Courtaulds' investment and Botany which were among the largest and most successful of all pre-1914 European direct investments in the U.S.A. Unlike the chemical industry, however, there is another important aspect of European influence on the American textile industry that should be mentioned: migration of actual industry occurred as well as the migration of capital. An example was the lace industry where whole sections migrated. The two main reasons for this were the imposition of tariffs by the U.S.A. and the encouragement of the emigration of workers by the trade unions because of unemployment at home. It is not clear whether this move always involved the closure of a firm's U.K. operation, although on many occasions it did. What is clear, however, is that British skills in some form dominated the U.S. silk, cotton and linen, thread, lace, hosiery, carpet and woollen industries up until about 1900. In other industries, such as Sheffield cutlery, the story is similar.

4.4 THE OIL INDUSTRY

The start of the American oil industry occurred in the 1850s and only 6 years after the world's first well was drilled in north-west Pennsylvania in 1859, the English Petroleum and Mining Company was organised with £50,000 capital to develop a tract of Pennsylvania land, but the company 'was soon lost in obscurity'.[29]

Areas where Direct Investment Occurred 1870–1917

By 1870 the U.S. oil industry had acquired the two characteristics that seem to predispose foreign enterprise towards investment: it was selling two-thirds of its output overseas; and it had achieved a considerable degree of concentration and skill at home.[30] However, what was still lacking, and would be 30 years in coming, was a willingness to assume the costs and risks of oil production in a foreign country although the incentives to make such an investment grew steadily after 1870. It was not until the advent of the automobile that foreign oil companies gained a real place in the U.S.A.

In 1912 the Shell Transport and Trading Company which was established in the U.K. in 1897 (see Chapter 5), started its first U.S. company, the American Gasoline Company (Philadelphia). In 1907 Shell merged with the Royal Dutch Company to form the Royal Dutch Shell Group. In 1912, to counteract Standard Oil's activities in the Far East, Royal Dutch Shell invaded the U.S. West Coast market with oil from Indonesia, having, in 1912, bought oil-producing land in Oklahoma from the British-controlled Dundee Corporation. In 1913 the company bought Californian Oilfields Ltd, made it into a subsidiary and renamed it Shell of California in 1914. That year it is estimated that Shell's U.S. holdings were more than $17.7 million.[31] In 1913 the Fremont Oil Co. Ltd, also a U.K. concern, bought Texas Oilfields Ltd, another U.K. company. The Fremont Oil Co. Ltd was capitalised at $200,000, but 'disappeared from the records' 5 years later. Another U.K. investment, the Oklahoma Oil and Refining Co. Ltd, started in 1910 and folded during World War I, but the Kern River Oilfields of California Ltd, and the Kansas, Oklahoma Oil and Refining Co. Ltd, founded in 1912, seem to have fared better in so far as they were still active after 1918.[32]

French, Belgian and Dutch groups financed the development of some major Wyoming oilfields at the end of the war. The French, however, sold their pre-war interests in Union des Petroles d'Oklahoma to the Pure Oil Company of the U.S.A. and also sold their interests in the very large Midwest Refining Company, which had 6 foreign directors out of a total of 14. This company eventually absorbed all other French Wyoming properties; the French shares were sold at $40 per share (nearly 80,000 shares) to Standard Oil of Indiana, which was one of the outcomes of the dissolution of the Standard Oil Trust. The major foreign oil companies identified by Lewis are listed in Table 4.1.

It is interesting to look at the response of the American companies during the period from the 1870s onward. Dutch producers in Sumatra began to challenge the American exporters in their Asian markets, while in Europe Russian and Rumanian producers stepped up the competition.

TABLE 4.1 Foreign-owned oil companies in the U.S.A., 1914 and 1919
(£ thousands unless otherwise stated)

Registration date and company		1914 Capital stock	1914 Funded debt	1919 Capital stock	1919 Funded debt	Notes
1907	Pacific Oilfields	250.0	—	250.0	—	
1910	Kern River Oilfields of California	497.0	—	597.2	—	
	Oklahoma Oil	102.0	—	—	—	Last mentioned 1918
	Premier Petroleum	$3,000.0	—	—	—	Last mentioned 1917
1911	Santa Maria Oilfields	1,160.0	—	287.0	—	Reorganised 1919
	Union des Petroles d'Oklahoma	fr.40,000.0	—	—	—	Control bought from French 1918
1912	Kansas, Oklahoma Oil & Refining	377.5	—	377.5	—	
	Shell of California	$17,716.0	—	$33,534.7	—	Dutch and British
1914	Freemont Oil	43.0	—	—	—	Last mentioned 1918
1917	Roxana Petroleum	—	—	$5,000.0	—	Dutch and British
	TOTAL	$40,864.5	—	$46,093.2	—	

All companies are British unless mentioned
Source: Lewis (1938), p. 565.

Until about 1900, the American policy was to try to gain control over the marketing outlets in the areas in question rather than to gain control of crude oil sources themselves. Although this tactic worked well enough at home, by 1900 it was evident that it was not suitable abroad. Standard Oil, which effectively represented the American industry, could not prevent foreign competition from simply by-passing Standard's distribution networks abroad by setting up its own. In the U.S.A. Standard could, until the advent of Shell, stop this happening by vicious price-cutting policies, and from 1900 there was a fundamental shift in strategy towards the control of the supply of crude oil and the extensive vertical integration of production, processing, transportation and marketing.

Shell's investment in California, which was largely the result of the failure of the international oil cartel in the Far East, or rather Standard Oil's policy of ignoring it,[33] was by far the largest European investment in the U.S. oil industry that was not either absorbed or forced out of business by the American companies.

4.5 THE BREWING AND LIQUOR INDUSTRY

U.K. investors showed a tremendous interest in U.S. brewing companies at the end of the 1880s. By 1889, 14 syndicates were registered in the U.K. for the purchase of U.S. companies. Their combined capital was $36.4 million. Although there were no new companies formed, by 1889 there were 23 British-owned brewing and liquor companies operating in the U.S.A. and their issued capital was $75 million.[34] Most of the controlled companies were consolidations, so in reality there were many more than 23, and in many cases the bought companies had interests, if not actual control in further companies. It would seem that over 100 companies could have been involved. British-owned breweries and liquor companies were located coast to coast across the U.S.A.

Two interesting points emerge. First, most British investment involved the takeover of American plants already in operation, in contrast to the general trend observed in early direct investment of establishing 'greenfield' ventures from scratch. Second, in their heyday many foreign firms were 'remarkably profitable'.[35] The F. W. Cook Brewing Co. Ltd, registered in England in 1892, had the following dividend pay-out rate: 20 per cent in 1914; 25 per cent in 1915; 30 per cent in 1916 and 12.5 per cent in 1917. The Goebal Brewing Co. Ltd, registered in England in 1889, paid 20 per cent in each of the 4 years 1910, 1911, 1913 and 1914, and 15 per cent in 1912. However, the majority of firms were paying little or no return to their owners by the time prohibition became law.[36]

Further estimates of the extent to which U.K. investors were involved in the U.S. brewing industry in the early 1900s have been given by Sir George Paish[37] and Cleona Lewis. Paish estimated that the amount of capital subscribed in London for investment in the U.S. industry had reached $55.9 million by 1910, and Lewis gave a figure of $58 million for the assets of the 17 U.K. companies operating in the U.S.A. in 1914, although British estimates of losses from the 1919 'bone-dry' constitutional amendment were $150 million (1919). Lewis also gave a figure of $5 million as the German equivalent for the 12 companies that they had operating there. These two estimates, allowing for the lack of new investment between 1910 and 1914, seem reasonably consistent.

By 1894, however, the bubble had burst and the main wave of U.K. investment in breweries was really over. The results of the majority of companies had been disappointing and although many had paid good dividends for 2 or 3 years, most had, by that time, reduced them or even curtailed payment altogether. Shares in brewing companies were mostly below par and often worthless, and by 1907 those companies still operating could only produce an average profit of 1½ per cent. Many companies had failed in the meantime and Coram[38] identified 4 reasons for the poor performance and subsequent failures.

(1) The syndicates had to pay excessive prices for the breweries and certainly more than the Americans would have done, e.g. the St Louis Brewery valued at $8.7 million was bought for $13.9 million.
(2) The U.K. investors bought at a boom period in the trade which collapsed shortly afterwards. In 1889 it was reported that half the 72 breweries in the vicinity of New York could have met the demand. Out of the 72 breweries, 11 were U.K.-owned. The local owners obviously saw the syndicates as an opportunity to sell out their interests and stay on at a high salary before the bubble burst.
(3) The syndicates tended to go for 100 per cent control and thereby removed the dual incentives of money-making and security from the retained management.
(4) An industry such as brewing requires local knowledge so foreign investors' attempts to impose control from a distance resulted in failure.

The brewing industry was one in which the investment was syndicate rather than direct and was only a very short-lived success. It appears that many of those investments that survived in 1914 were liquidated during

TABLE 4.2 Foreign-owned breweries in the U.S.A., 1914 and 1919
(£ thousands unless otherwise stated)

Registration date and company		1914 Capital stock	1914 Funded debt	1919 Capital stock	1919 Funded debt	Notes
1888	New York Breweries	380.0	349.7	380.0	296.0	
1889	Bartholomay Brewing	743.5	463.0	743.5	463.0	
	Chicago Breweries	400.0	216.6	400.0	165.8	
	Cincinnati Breweries	68.7	152.2	68.7	152.2	
	Goebel Brewing	103.7	–	–	–	Liquidated 1919
	Indianapolis Breweries	270.0	160.0	270.0	197.8	
	Jones (Frank) Brewing	600.0	517.5	–	–	In receivership 1919
	St Louis Breweries	1,800.0	450.0	1,800.0	337.6	
	Washington	127.6	26.0	–	–	Liquidated 1915
1890	City of Chicago Brewing & Malting	1,250.0	–	1,250.0	–	
	Milwaukee & Chicago Breweries	852.5	82.2	852.5	82.2	
	New England Breweries	410.0	174.1	410.0	194.0	
	San Francisco Breweries	171.0	553.2	171.0	592.3	
	Springfield Breweries	100.0	15.0	100.0	15.0	
1892	Cook (F.W.) Brewing	130.0	70.0	78.0	–	
1899	Denver United Breweries	400.0	168.3	400.0	168.3	
	TOTAL	$38,035.0	$16,989.0	$34,618.5	$13,321.0	

All companies are British-owned.
Source: Lewis (1938), p. 565.

World War I and certainly none survive today. Table 4.2 shows Lewis's estimates of foreign activity in brewing. Davies suggested that 'British capital and enterprise have, from the beginning, regarded beer and spirits as a sort of public utility with which every country ought to be endowed'.[39] British capital was instrumental in promoting combinations of breweries and rationalising the industry.

4.6 THE MINING AND ALLIED INDUSTRIES

Before the late 1800s nearly all investment in this type of industry was portfolio but a switch to direct investment then took place because of the high failure rate of the companies. Much less syndicate money was involved than in the brewing industry but nevertheless several large companies were founded. In 1877 the Southern States Coal Iron and Land Company was established. This company built a whole small town at South Pittsburg, Tennessee and started a blast furnace operation there.[40] Before long, however, the U.K. interests were sold out to the Americans.

Many instances of British capital and some interest from Dutch, French, German and Belgian investors can be found in mining investments of various degrees of speculative endeavour. Capital involvement usually did not imply control from the investing country, even where joint stock companies were established to exploit the mines. Overcapitalisation was a frequent problem and speculative booms with inflated prices more often benefited middlemen marketing shares rather than either mine operators or final investors. Some management direction on broad policy issues may have been transmitted from Europe but in most instances a single man was in charge of operations at the site — very few foreign-controlled mining enterprises managed to combine adequate working capital, capable management, impartial control and a producing mine free of legal problems. The term 'direct investment' can be applied to very few mining companies of the pre-World War I era. Control of raw materials through to finished goods in a fully vertically integrated company was, except in the oil industry, a between-the-wars creation. From 1860 to 1901 total investment in Western mines by the U.K. alone is estimated at between £40 and £50 million by Spence.[41] Waves of profit-seeking speculation in portfolio ventures were directed from the U.K., and Western mines provided an attractive sink when well marketed. This was not, however, organised or controlled directly from the source country.

U.K. interests founded the largest iron works in the country in Rock-

Areas where Direct Investment Occurred 1870–1917

bridge County, Virginia in 1881, and in 1895 the Otis Steel Company in Cleveland, Ohio was purchased with U.K. capital.[42] In spite of this the company continued to be run quite successfully by Americans, and was the only one that remained in British hands for a long period. It was sold back in 1919 for $13 million – the initial investment had been $4.5 million.

At one time, the Olympia Portland Cement Co. Ltd, was also U.K.-controlled. Around 1889, $10 million was invested by the British in Watts Iron and Steel Company at Middlesboro, Kentucky and at the start of World War I, U.K. investors controlled the Ducktown Sulphur, Copper and Iron Company, established in 1891, and Borax Consolidated Ltd, established in 1889.

Belgian interests controlled the Belgian–Bohemian Mining Company and the Jualin Alaska Mines. German interests controlled the American Metal Company, established in 1887. This company soon diversified into smelters, refineries, chemical manufacturing, coalmining and shipping.[43] (See also Section 4.10.)

The Exploration Company Ltd, was controlled by British investors and the Rothschilds of France, who bought a quarter interest in Anaconda in 1895. The company owned several technically sophisticated British exploration and development companies operating in the U.S.A. The Boston Consolidated Gold and Copper Mining Company Ltd, founded in England in 1898, was absorbed in the Utah Copper Company in 1910 and became a major source of copper after solving the problems of extracting 'porphyry' coppers and reducing their ores.[44]

There were many other U.K. investments in exploration companies but the history is very confused and the amount and type of capital involvement vague. It is doubtful if any of them would be covered by today's accepted definition of direct investment. Examples of success in terms of financial return are easy to find – The Tom Boy Gold Mines Ltd (U.K.-owned) paid dividends equal to 225 per cent of its capital between 1810 and 1917 and De Lamar Mining Co. Ltd, also British, paid dividends equal to 146 per cent on its initial investment between 1891 and 1910 as well as repatriating some capital. Many more were disastrous and made huge losses. Table 4.3 summarises Lewis's findings – but by 1914 many briefly flowering mining ventures had disappeared or been absorbed by U.S. companies.

TABLE 4.3 Foreign-owned mining companies in the U.S.A., 1914 and 1919 (£ thousands unless otherwise stated)

Registration date and company	1914 Capital stock	1914 Funded debt	1919 Capital stock	1919 Funded debt	Notes
1884 Arizona Copper Co. Ltd	1,736.5	400.0	1,736.5	–	Acquired by Phelps Dodge Corporation in 1921
1891 Ducktown Sulphur, Copper & Iron	200.0	120.0	200.0	74.8	
1895 Alaska United	$575.0	–	$575.0	–	
1896 Mountain Copper	–	750.0	–	625.0	
1899 Arizona Consolidated Copper Mines Ltd	135.0	–	135.0	–	Liquidated 1922
Borax Consolidated	460.0	1,064.0	460.0	1,064.0	
Stratton's Independence	125.0	–	–	–	Last mentioned 1917
1899 Tom Boy Gold Mines	310.0	–	310.0	–	
1900 Camp Bird	$574.8	–	–	–	
1901 De Lamar Company	80.0	–	–	–	Last mentioned 1916
1903 Minerals Separation Ltd	50.0	–	–	–	American rights bought by American Co. in 1916
1904 Vibro Syndicate	66.0	–	–	–	Last mentioned 1917
1905 Oroville Dredging	$3,432.6	–	–	–	Liquidated 1919–20
1906 Silverfields	149.1	–	–	–	Last mentioned 1915
1909 Mary Murphy	$1,790.5	$231.0	$1,790.5	$169.0	
1910 Frontenac Consolidated Mines	278.0	28.5	–	–	Liquidated 1916
Sterling Coal Co. Ltd	$12,130.0	$1,560.0	$2,130.0	$1,430.0	Canadian
1912 Southern Aluminum	$5,500.0	–	–	–	Bought by Americans in 1915 from the French
1913 St John Mines	75.0	–	75.0	–	
1914 Plymouth Consolidated Gold Mines	240.0	–	240.0	–	
Natomas Company of California	$9,249.5	$9,049.1	$9,249.5	$10,592.4	
Wah Chang Mining & Smelting Co. Ltd	–	–	$2,000.0	–	Chinese
Crescent Mining Co. Ltd	$1,000.0	–	$1,708.0	–	Canadian
TOTAL	$43,775.4	$22,652.6	$33,235.5	$21,010.4	

All companies are British unless stated.
Source: Lewis (1938), p. 564.

4.7 THE LAND DEVELOPMENT INDUSTRY

A good example of the way foreign investors came to own land is the Alabama Coal, Iron, Land and Colonization Co., established in England in 1882. It administered and developed land which its owners had acquired when Alabama defaulted on 8 per cent 1870 bonds in 1876. This company still held nearly 500,000 acres in 1914 and consistently paid dividends of over 25 per cent.[45] Most of the land that came into British hands did so in this way or through land acquired for railways, and it was frequently held for appreciation or sold to immigrants. One exception was the Fine Cotton Spinners & Doublers Association Ltd, which held land in the South as an investment for profit in agricultural developments such as cotton and fruit and for access to coal and timber.

Lewis[46] estimates that a few years before World War I, between 30 and 35 million acres were controlled by European interests, mainly British. Huge areas of land were required for cattle raising and Lewis found that not less than 18 companies were registered in the U.K. to raise cattle in the U.S.A. in the period 1880–90. Their total investment was more than $27 million in over 4 million acres. Many did well, including the Prairie Cattle Co. Ltd, which was the first, founded in 1880 by a syndicate called the Scottish American Mortgage Company; Prairie Cattle paid dividends of 20.5 per cent in 1883.[47] By 1900 nearly 50 per cent of the European companies had folded. Initial investment in 29 land companies which Lewis identified as foreign (registered 1897–1911) was $52 million – 14 were still active in 1914 with an aggregate capitalisation of more than $40 million. (There must have been many omissions, however, for in 1909 the *Philadelphia Bulletin* published a list of 54 foreign holdings, only one of which was included in Lewis's 29.[48])

Of the 13 original U.K.-owned meat-packing houses (two in Cincinnati dated from 1842 and developed in anticipation of a reduction in British tariffs), only five were still active in 1917. Most were sold to U.S. interests such as Swift & Co., which bought into the Anglo-American Provision Co. and purchased the Kansas City plant of G. Fowler & Son & Co. in 1902.

The number of foreign-owned land companies reached a peak in the middle 1880s and attracted a great deal of unfavourable comment and political opposition – not only to foreign absentee owners, but also to Eastern capitalists. Absentee (particularly foreign) landlords were the butt of the Granger Movement and one of the aims of the Populist platform in 1892 was their removal. This resentment is traced in detail by Crapoi, who notes that resentment against British capitalists was greatest in enterprises connected with land and land-ownership: 'such enterprises as cattle ranches, grain elevators, farms, cotton plantations, irrigation projects, railroads, stockyards, mine and land companies'.[49] It has been estimated that over 1500 British companies were doing business in the Trans-Mississippi West during the last half of the nineteenth century. The livestock industry, more than any other, bore the brunt of the anti-British feeling. The passing of 'Alien Land Acts' in a number of states throughout the 1890s reflected the 'America for the Americans' emotions.[50]

TABLE 4.4 Foreign-owned land companies in the U.S.A., 1914 and 1919 (£ thousands unless otherwise stated)

Registration date and company	1914 Capital stock	1914 Funded debt	1919 Capital stock	1919 Funded debt	Notes
1879 Platte Land	34.0	–	–	–	Liquidated 1919
Missouri Land	15.9	–	11.9	–	
1882 Alabama Coal, Iron Land & Colonisation	36.9	–	36.9	–	
North American Land & Timber	90.4	–	90.4	–	
1884 Mount Carbon	73.8	29.4			Last mentioned 1918
1885 Capital Freehold Land and Investment	1,350.8	–	–	–	Liquidated 1918/19
1889 Trust & Mortgage of Iowa	175.0	379.1	175.0	373.9	
1890 Riverside Orange	471.8	49.8	–	–	Liquidated 1915
1892 Rugby, Tennessee	128.4	–	–	–	Last mentioned 1916
1894 San Jacinto Land	34.3	21.7	34.3	21.7	
1900 United Railway & Trading	390.8	725.0	–	–	Last mentioned 1916
1905 New York City Freehold Estates	613.5	40.0	375.0	228.0	
1907 United States Lumber & Cotton	$3,457.9	–	$3,482.9		
1911 San Antonio Land	$8,000.0	$1,200.0	–		In receivership (1938)
(All companies above are British)					
Also: New York Water Front	–	–	$2,000.0		Bought by French Government in World War I, sold to Americans in 1930 for $2,000,000
TOTAL	$28,535.9	$12,225.0	$9,100.4	$13,118.0	

Tables 4.4 and 4.5 list the foreign land companies and cattle companies traced by Lewis. Note the many liquidations 1914–19.

The Matador Land and Cattle Company owned by Harmsworth, Mckay, Irons & Co. of Scotland held nearly a million acres of Texas land and reputedly had the largest herd of Herefords anywhere in the world. They also held citrus and cattle land in Florida.[51] The longevity and success of the Matador Land and Cattle Company may be due to its policy direction from Dundee, to firm organisational structure and to the fact that during the 65 years of Scottish ownership, only five men held the top management positions and only five men served as superintendent in the ranch itself.[52] Many (Scottish) textile firms accepted real estate instead of cash payment at the height of the Civil War (1861–5). One failed company was the Handsworth Land and Cattle Company incorporated in 1883 and directed by five Dundee merchants which did so badly in the first 5 years of ranching on the prairies that it rapidly gave up paying dividends and reduced its capital.

Despite the romanticism which surrounds the English and Scottish cattle and land companies, they do not readily fulfil the definitions of direct investment. Although in some cases control was firmly exercised from the U.K., the investments were carried out by individuals or syndicates rather than by companies extending their business from Europe. The target was investment in the U.S.A. when and where land was cheap so this was akin to a portfolio flow, since capital organised for the purpose flowed to the area where the host (not the source) country had the advantage. The original objective was to export meat, tallow and leather back to the U.K. in anticipation of threats to the home markets from U.S. products. The expansion of the domestic U.S. market largely substituted for such possibilities.

TABLE 4.5 Foreign-owned cattle companies in the U.S.A., 1914 and 1919 (£ thousands unless otherwise stated)

Registration date and company	1914		1919		Notes
	Capital stock	Funded debt	Capital stock	Funded debt	
1880 Prairie Cattle		70.0	–	–	Last mentioned 1915
1882 California Pastoral & Agricultural	165.0	98.8	–	–	Last mentioned 1914
Matador Land & Cattle	200.0	164.9	200.0	154.6	Sold to New York Investment Bankers 1951
1883 Swan Land & Cattle	250.0	–	150.0	24.8	Scottish control diluted 1911, 1924, finally 1956
1884 American Pastoral	49.7	–	–	–	Last mentioned 1916
TOTAL	$3,323.5	$1,618.5	$1,750.0	$897.0	

All companies are British-owned.
Source: Lewis (1938), p. 562. W. T. Jackson (1968), *The Enterprising Scot*, Edinburgh University Press. W. M. Pearce (1964), *The Matador Land and Cattle Company*, Oklahoma University Press.

A further, short-lived, venture into the U.S.A. land-holding for a rather different reason was made by the U.K. safety match manufacturers, Bryant & May.[53] William Bryant and Francis May went into partnership in 1840 importing Swedish matches before acquiring the patent for safety matches (which they started producing in an old crinoline factory in Bow, London, in 1855). The company was incorporated in 1884, since it had gained virtual control of U.K. match manufacture. Here, as elsewhere, international rivalry began at an early stage and their main competitors were the U.S.-owned Diamond Match Company.

Early in 1902 the Managing Director of Bryant & May visited the U.S.A. When he returned to the U.K. he recommended that 'the proposal of the Diamond Match Company of Illinois to one-half share in their entire Californian Timber Scheme on even terms be accepted'. A Bryant & May Ltd Directors' resolution dated 9 September 1902 recorded the decision that a separate company be formed in the U.S.A. to protect this joint holding. This company was established with an initial capital of $1 million to be held equally by the two companies with three directors appointed from the boards of each parent company to the new company's board.

Initially, the transaction seems to have been successful. In June 1903 Bryant & May's Board noted an agreement with the Southern Pacific Railroad Company to build a new railroad line – presumably a siding to a sawmill. There also seems to have been a further such agreement between the Diamond Match Company and the Butte County Railroad Company. Payments were made on account to the Southern Pacific and progress seems to have been made in view of a letter outlining the 'timber lands acquired and controlled to date'.[54]

Although information is sparse, it seems that the transaction must have gone sour. In a Minute of the Board of Bryant & May dated 9 April 1908, the decision was made to sell the U.K. company's interest in Californian properties at cost plus interest at the rate of 5 per cent per annum from the time of payment of the cost to 31 December 1907 or the date the money was received. The progress of the sale is duly noted in later Minutes and the land divested. Interestingly, Diamond Match Company disposed of all its assets in Europe on 8 June 1914, presumably fearing the effect of the imminent war.

Like many other European investments in land-holding, Bryant & May's was short-lived. Clearly, its intention was to integrate vertically and control supplies of its critical raw material. Whether the divestment was due to difficulties of control at a distance, or disappointment in supplies, or even failure of transport arrangements, we can only surmise – or indeed whether the arrangements with its erstwhile competitor in control of inputs was the basic cause.

Areas where Direct Investment Occurred 1870–1917

The portfolio investments in the U.S. railroads and direct investments in land were instrumental in European capital becoming involved in finance and insurance which were essential to them. However, in itself, European direct involvement in U.S. land was often unintentional and the land usually did not long remain out of American hands.

4.8 THE FLOUR-MILLING INDUSTRY

British investors, as a syndicate, put $9.3 million into the Pillsbury-Washburn Flour Mills Co. Ltd organised in England in 1889. This company was formed by a merger of two others as part of the deal after profits had been cut during a period of severe competition and it was one of the very few flour-milling enterprises to involve European capital. For a time it operated six flour mills in and around Minneapolis and was instrumental in introducing new technology, including wheat testing and mixing.[55]

The previous owners retained a substantial interest (and effective management control) in the new company, which in addition to milling had outside involvements in water power and wheat elevator companies. At that time it was the largest milling company in the world. However, the results were disappointing: dividends on common stock were paid in only 2 of its first 8 years, and in 1908 the company went into receivership after lack of investment had downgraded quality and the equipment had been allowed to deteriorate. The English stockholders found it impossible to secure the necessary capital to put the company on its feet so they were forced to accept a plan offered by the Pillsbury family, who had a substantial interest, and A. C. Loring, one of the receivers. A new company was formed to lease the Pillsbury mills but by this time the U.K. interest had dropped to a token 2.5 per cent. The new company prospered, and in 1924 the remaining 2.5 per cent was bought out, when re-financing resulted in the absorption of the Pillsbury-Washburn Company by the Pillsbury Flour Mills Company.

The reasons for the failure of the original company would seem to have been ineffective administration from the U.K., inability to pay dividends on over-heavy capitalisation, industrial trouble in 1903, and losses incurred by speculation on the U.S. wheat market (which were apparently concealed from stockholders).[56] The English company was not popular in Minneapolis and its attempts in the 1890s to absorb the nearby C. C. Washburn mills were beaten off, to the delight of the locals. Defensive combinations of local firms were formed at this time.

4.9 THE TOBACCO INDUSTRY

Before the beginning of the twentieth century, the nature of competition in the tobacco industry was determined by U.K.–U.S.A. rivalry. The U.S. industry was dominated by the famous U.S. Trust, Consolidated Tobacco, made up of American Tobacco (cigarettes) and the Continental Tobacco Corporation (chewing plug tobacco), built up by James Buchanan Duke after American Tobacco was formed in 1889. Duke's attempt to enter the British industry by a takeover of the U.K. company, Ogden Ltd, and to cut prices to British jobbers in 1901 led 13 U.K. companies to merge in 1902 to form the Imperial Tobacco Company (shortly afterwards they were joined by five more companies), which was felt to be strong enough to resist the American challenge.[57] As a result of negotiations to end the ensuing stalemate, the British–American Tobacco Company (BAT) was formed.

Duke's entry via the purchase of Ogden's led Imperial directors to visit the U.S.A. in 1902 with instructions to buy up any tobacco business free of Duke's Trust. They were particularly concerned that supplies of leaf tobacco should not be cut off as a result of American Tobacco's extensive backward integration.[58]

This brief period of uncertainty was ended in September 1902 when the Imperial Directors entered into 'two historic agreements' with Consolidated Tobacco.[59] The first provided that Ogden's should be transferred back to British control by Imperial's purchase. The second provided that the export and overseas trade of both Imperial and American Tobacco was transferred to a new company to be formed in the U.K. – BAT.

The results (as described by Corina) were:

(1) American Tobacco withdrew from the U.K. market and agreed not to re-enter it and Imperial agreed not to enter the U.S. market.
(2) Each of the two companies acquired the trading rights in the other's brands in its home market, including the right to use the respective trade marks.
(3) The two companies agreed not to engage in exports except through BAT, and BAT was thus entitled to purchase at a price not exceeding cost any export business afterwards acquired by either Imperial or American Tobacco; any shares in foreign companies which might be acquired by either, and the export business and the assets employed in any such business of any company, the direct or indirect control of

Areas where Direct Investment Occurred 1870–1917

which might be acquired by either Imperial or American Tobacco.
(4) Imperial was allotted one-third, and American Tobacco two-thirds, of BAT's equity capital — both appointed Directors to the Board.
(5) BAT was bound not to trade in the U.K. or U.S. markets.
(6) American Tobacco acquired (through the sale of Ogden) a substantial minority interest in Imperial and the right to nominate three Directors to Imperial's Board.[60]

The days of such grandiose worldwide market sharing were limited and after a drawn-out 4-year action, in May 1911 the United States Supreme Court held the U.S. Trust as acting in restraint of trade. President Roosevelt's motives in pursuing this action seem not to have been solely based on economics, as he held a personal grudge against Duke for his activities in trying to turn the Republican party against Teddy's nomination in 1904. However, the trust was broken up and American Tobacco was forced to sell or distribute its share in BAT. American Tobacco's large shareholding in Imperial (about 14 per cent) was diluted. Imperial was now free to sell in the U.S.A. any brands not on the list which American Tobacco had sold in the U.S.A. prior to the anti-trust suit. Imperial retained trading rights to some American Tobacco brands in the U.K. The division of markets between Imperial and BAT was retained — neither cherished the desire to enter the U.S. market. It was not until 1927 that BAT entered the U.S. market by purchasing Brown and Williamson.[61]

Outside the trust, the Philip Morris tobacco house, in consultation with its sole American agent (Gustave Eckmeyer, New York), decided to push English brands in the U.S. market and in 1902 established the first Philip Morris Corporation in New York. One of its principal listed assets was a brand sold in London called Marlboro — destined to be one of the world's largest-selling cigarettes.[62] Seven years later, the British owners of Philip Morris re-incorporated and in 1919 a new concern, Philip Morris & Company, was formed in Virginia — Philip Morris Inc. now is a U.S. international holding company.

4.10 THE METAL INDUSTRY

Before 1914 German interests, operating in conjunction with but dominating local financial interests, largely controlled the world's trading and industry in a number of base metals.[63]

In 1887 the American Metal Company was founded in New York, when it became apparent that the U.S. market would be of major importance to the well-established German group, Metallgesellschaft. This firm was already represented in the U.S.A. through the New York bank, Landenburg, Thalmann & Co. in an agreement dating from the 1870s. The new company, American Metal Co. was funded by Metallgesellschaft, the London-based firm Merton and the New York bank, although Landenburgh, Thalmann & Co's participation soon diminished while Metallgesellschaft's increased. One of the leading Directors and President of American Metal Company was J. Longeloth, a former member of the German company's Board.

American Metal Co., which only had an initial share capital of $100,000, was soon in a position to pay out huge dividends and by 1896 its 'reserves' already exceeded the initial capital invested. The company had to increase its capitalisation every other year. So strong was the company that the depression of the U.S. economy at the turn of the century had little effect on its progress. A St Louis branch was established to service the growing Mid-West market. Junior executives were despatched from Frankfurt to the U.S.A. to facilitate the firm's expansion. The company diversified with the support of the parent companies in London and Frankfurt.[64] At the outbreak of hostilities the Alien Property Custodian seized its assets. Wrangling over the rightful ownership of these assets continued until 1938. Aaron Hirsch und Sohn had control over subsidiaries in the U.S.A. in addition to its association with Metallgesellschaft. Subsidiaries of Beer Sondheimer and L. Vogelstein were two other German firms involved in the metal industry and had assets which were listed as being seized during World War I by the Alien Property Custodian.

In 1915 France sold its $5.5 million investment in the Southern Aluminum Co. and its $6.6 million investment in the Utah Copper Co., the latter to Kennecott Copper Corporation.

In 1919 the British Otis Steel Co., which had been operating in Ohio since 1895, was sold to American interests for $13 million. Both the Watts Iron and Steel Company, founded in 1889 with a capital of $3 million in Middlesboro, Kentucky, and the Southern States Coal, Iron and Land Company, which founded the town of New Pittsburg, were British financed.[65] These transactions all indicate active involvement in the U.S.A. before 1914 by other nations, but the Germans were the main European investors with a substantial stake in the U.S.A. that only ceased with the confiscations of their subsidiaries during World War I.

4.11 THE TIN-PLATE INDUSTRY

Prior to 1890, 70 per cent of all the South Wales production of tin-plate had been bought by the U.S.A., but the McKinley Tariff of 1890, at a rate of 90 per cent *ad valorem*, virtually wiped out the business. Both before and after 1890 various attempts by immigrant Welsh workers to set up a tin-plate industry in the U.S.A. failed. After 1890, several of the affected companies attempted to transfer their operations to the U.S.A. and many more closed completely.

The craft system was, however, not suitable for the U.S. requirements, and rapid consolidation of these small ventures culminated in 1898 with the formation of the American Tin Plate Co. The company had a capital of $50 million and control of 39 production units.[66] At this time any remaining Welsh financial interest effectively ceased.

4.12 THE SILK INDUSTRY

The silk industry in the U.K. suffered a similar demise to that of the tin-plate industry. In 1884 a 60 per cent *ad valorem* duty on all imports was imposed by the U.S.A. The U.K. industry had already been dealt a blow by the Anglo-French Cobden Treaty of 1860 which allowed French silk into the U.K. duty-free. One attempt to salvage something from these two disasters was the formation of the American Velvet Co. shortly afterwards. Over the next 25 years, however, many small firms and their workers emigrated to the U.S.A. It has been estimated that during that time 16,000 people from the Macclesfield area alone moved to the U.S.A.[67] It does not appear that any of these ventures achieved any significance and most were taken over by American interests before long.

4.13 THE ELECTRICAL INDUSTRY

The chemical and electrical industries, as shown by Faith,[68] were the sectors in which continental enterprises had their oldest and strongest innovative advantages and have accounted for the bulk of continental companies' U.S. operations since the 1880s. Even so, the number of ventures in both fields before 1914 was small, particularly in the electrical field. One of the first to occur was in 1904 when A.E.G. (Allegemeine Elektrizitaets Gesellschaft) of Germany combined finances with the American Union Electric Company to further technical and sales co-operation between the two companies.[69]

In 1889 A.E.G. had been a member of the German syndicate involved in the creation of the Edison General Electric Co.[70] This was somewhat ironic because Edison and General Electric's Thomson Houston Company had helped to start A.E.G. initially. De Witt & Hertz and Siemens & Halske (see Chapter 5) were also leaders in establishing companies in the U.S.A. although the latter's was not a success.

In the automobile electrical industry, the Bosch Magneto Co. and the Eiseman Magneto Co. were both offshoots of German firms and prior to 1914 produced half of all the magnetos sold in the U.S.A.[71] At the time they were seized, German investment in them was not less than $11.5 million.

The electrical industry, in common with the dyestuff industry, was an area where U.K. influence was relatively small. The greatest European influence was that of Germany, but in spite of the seizure of all its subsidiaries in 1917, its success prior to that time does not appear to have been very marked.

4.14 THE AUTOMOBILE INDUSTRY

Before 1914 there was very little foreign investment in car manufacturing in the U.S.A. There was, however, a considerable export trade from Europe to the U.S.A. In Europe, the machines of Benz and Daimler appeared on German roads in 1886 and 1888 respectively and in 1888 the Daimler Motor Co. was founded in New York.[72] Steinway, already well-known in the piano business, was the principal American partner in the joint venture. At first the company imported Daimler cars from Germany as well as Panhard and Levassor cars from France, but in 1893 Daimler began production of its handcrafted luxury cars in Britain and followed this, a few years later, with production in the U.S.A.[73] The American venture was a 'Mercedes' similar to the imported one but 25 per cent cheaper.[74]

Fiat (see Chapter 5) also manufactured in the U.S.A. prior to 1914 in Poughkeepsie, New York. In 1919, Rolls-Royce began to produce cars at

Springfield, Massachusetts. The Daimler and Fiat operations were both joint ventures and fairly short-lived — the Daimler plant closed in 1913 after a fire — but had this not happened, it would have been confiscated in 1917 and German interest would have ceased only 4 years later than it actually did. In neither the Daimler nor the Fiat case did the investments attain much significance although both were quite successful for a time.

4.15 THE RAILWAY INDUSTRY

Although financed by vast amounts of portfolio capital from Europe (mainly the U.K.), the American railroads were almost never controlled by their foreign shareholders or banks. As Jenks[75] put it:

> ... The U.S. provided its own enterprise, its own contractors, its own happy coincidences of private profit with objects of public concern but railway iron and working capital the U.S. could not provide as rapidly as its development required. Frankfurt and London made the acquaintance of a wide selection of bonds without having much of anything to do with railway management and promotion in the U.S.A.

Possible exceptions to this portfolio investment framework were the Atlantic and Great Western Railway from New York to Cincinnati which was financed by the U.K. and built by U.K. labour working for a U.K. construction firm, and the Oregon railroad built and owned by a Scottish company in 1879. It is not clear how much capital was involved in either case or where it originated.

Jenks notes that:

> the striking thing about all this purchase of railway securities is the small amount of British entrepreneurship, or business leadership or control that was involved ... there is no comparable case in the annals of foreign investment of a class of entrepreneurs of one country making so continuous and successful appeal to investors of another for a supply of capital on the unsupported credit of the prospects of companies which they, not the investors were to control.[76]

Jenks goes on to suggest that with the exception of railroads connected with land, timber or mining, only one railway system was organised, operated and expanded under the direct auspices of a British company

— the Alabama Great Southern. Known as the 'Queen and Crescent' system, it ran from Cincinnati to New Orleans and was disposed of piecemeal before 1924 to the Southern and Illinois Central. Large landownings were a source of profit and interest, but British attempts to exercise control were usually unsuccessful because of company structure, remoteness and dispersion of shareholders from management and lack of concern and competence amongst absentee owners.

However, control was often exercised and the investment protected by a 'close and continuing relationship between an American railway and a British finance house'.[77] In some cases, such as the Philadelphia and Reading, the British house actually owned a controlling amount of the shares. However, when control depended on banker–railroad relationships, there was always the possibility of the railway finding another banker. Also, control was sometimes exercised through a British investor sitting as a member on the American railway's board of directors.

The part played by the U.S. railways in the development of the U.S.A. was immense and, although not direct, the portfolio investment in the railways from Europe and particularly the U.K., was considerable. The regional configuration of 'British' railroads is revealing — they ran from the resource-rich South and Mid-West to the Eastern Seaboard.

4.16 FINANCE, MORTGAGE, INSURANCE AND BANKING COMPANIES

Although the finance industry is not included in manufacturing industry, it played a vital part in the development of other industries, and for that reason it should be examined.

One of the first investments made by a European country occurred in 1884 when Barings, the famous London merchant bank, bought Merchant Exchange of New York City. Many other foreign-owned financial institutions were established in the early 1800s in the eastern states of the U.S.A., and in the western states from about 1870. Many of these were mortgage companies set up to finance the land development schemes which were abundant at that time and three of the more successful ones singled out by McClain were the American Freehold-Land Mortgage Co. of London, established 1879; the Texas Land Mortgage Co. Ltd, established 1882; and the Oregon Mortgage Co. Ltd, established 1883. Lewis has estimated that 15 companies which were already registered in 1874

Areas where Direct Investment Occurred 1870–1917

originated in England (of which seven still survived at the start of World War I) with a capital of $45 million and debts outstanding of $110 million. In a similar exercise, about a dozen Dutch mortgage banks established after 1874 had loans outstanding of $40 million in 1916. The U.K. companies were mainly in the Pacific north-west and the Dutch in the Mid-West and West. At the beginning of World War I total foreign loans on U.S. real estate aggregated 'not less than' $200–$250 million.[78]

TABLE 4.6 Foreign-owned mortgage and finance companies in the U.S.A., 1914 and 1919 (£ thousands unless otherwise stated)

Registration date and company	1914		1919		Notes
	Capital stock	Funded debt	Capital stock	Funded debt	
1874 Scottish American Mortgage	1,275.2	637.5	1,275.2	451.0	
1879 American Freehold Land & Mortgage	358.0	902.6	358.0	828.7	
1882 Texas Land & Mortgage	165.0	569.3	165.0	529.3	
1883 Oregon Mortgage	325.0	325.0	325.0	223.1	
1886 Pacific Loan & Investment	187.5	539.5	187.5	406.9	
Land Mortgage Bank of Texas	827.9	400.0	827.9	400.0	
1897 Mortgage & Debenture	320.0	485.0	320.0	485.0	
1910 Investment Company for Electrical Enterprises	?	?	?	?	A Swiss Corporation
1919 French American Banking Corporation	–	–	$1,250.0	–	French : American 50/50
TOTAL	$17,293.0	$19,294.5	$18,543.0	$16,620.0	

All companies are British unless otherwise stated.
Source: Lewis (1938), p. 563.

The Phoenix was the first insurance branch office to open in the U.S.A. in 1804. It closed in 1810 but reopened in 1879. In the interim the Liverpool, London & Globe opened in the U.S.A. in 1848, the Royal Insurance Co. in 1851, the Northern Assurance Co. in 1854 and the British American Insurance Co. in 1874. In addition, the New York Life Assurance & Trust

Co., the American Life Assurance & Trust Co. and the Ohio Life Assurance & Trust Co. all had substantial foreign investments in them during the same period.[79] Some idea of the number of companies in which foreign investments were made has been given by Lewis, who determined that between 1861 and 1895 32 foreign insurance companies closed and between 1896 and 1915, 21 more branches were closed. Lewis's estimates for companies operating in 1914 and 1919 are shown in Table 4.6.

In banking, despite the strict control exercised by the 1830s state banking laws, British interests controlled the Manhattan Bank Co. in New York and there were substantial European interests in the Bank of North America and the second bank of the U.S.A., the Girard Bank of Philadelphia, before its closure in 1842, as well as in several others. Lloyds Bank established a branch in New York in 1880, Standard Chartered Bank in 1902 and Thomas Cook set up in New York as early as 1873.

Robert Fleming founded its New York Branch in 1869 and it is now one of the most successful banks in the lucrative and prestigious business of underwriting and managing new issues. Fleming masterminded the massive Scottish portfolio investment in the U.S.A. over a century ago.[80] Scottish portfolio capital was extremely important in British investment in the U.S.A. in this period (the late 1870s to the outbreak of World War I). Lenman and Donaldson note that:

> ... it has been estimated that Dundee, with an annual income of £1,500,000 on average in the eighteen-eighties, had invested £5,000,000 in the United States of America by about 1890. This was equivalent to nine or ten times the value of all the town's real estate, and was said to be equal to the savings of the town for twenty years. It was believed that in absolute terms Edinburgh invested more in the United States than Dundee, but it was believed that Dundee had a much higher proportion of its total resources devoted to American investment.[81]

This disproportionate contribution of Scotland was largely portfolio investment via the burgeoning, highly speculative investment trusts of the time.

It is not possible to identify the majority of these early interests as portfolio or direct investment and in any case they are not manufacturing concerns, but it is useful to have some idea of the scale on which foreign capital was involved in the U.S. financial sector at that time. Once again, the majority of the capital came from the U.K. but finance was one area where a considerable amount of Dutch capital was invested, particularly in mortgage companies.

4.17 OTHER INDUSTRIES

In addition to the various specific categories, many other European companies set up production units in the U.S.A. but it is often impossible to identify the type and source of the capital used.

In the U.S. leather industry, the Liverpool-based firm of Alfred Booth and Company became a major manufacturer, producing about one-eighth of the 240 million square feet of kid leather annually manufactured in the U.S.A. in the 10 years preceding World War I. The history of Booth's development in the U.S.A. is a fascinating transition from merchant to manufacturer and an illustration of the absence of division between ownership and management so prevalent in family-dominated firms of the time.[82]

Alfred Booth and Company were founded as a partnership between Alfred and Charles Booth in 1863 in Liverpool, England, as a merchant house and shipping agency. After completing his apprenticeship, Alfred Booth visited the U.S.A. in 1857 where he worked in the New York office of Rathbone & Company, a Liverpool merchant house (Liverpool and New York had very close economic ties). After a period of importing light leathers (sheep and goat skins) into the U.S.A. in partnership with a U.S. citizen called Walkden (who went insane), the partnership was dissolved and Alfred Booth & Co., Liverpool and Alfred Booth & Co., New York were formed. Initial difficulties in selling stock in the U.S.A. led to diversification into such activities as buying for cotton brokers, but these activities were mainly unsuccessful. Alfred Booth withdrew from active participation in the business in 1896 and Charles assumed leadership.

In 1881 the first Booth Steamship Company was formed and attempts were made to integrate shipping with leather importing. However, finished leather goods were virtually shut out of the U.S. market by high tariffs. In addition, difficulties in collecting debts owed to the Booth company across the Atlantic forced it to manufacture in both the U.K. and U.S.A. The growth of the Booth company started with a partner, two clerks and a warehouseman in 1867. In 1870, a Boston branch was opened in the centre of the U.S. boot and shoe trade and the increase in demand for boots and shoes in the U.S.A. 1860—90 led to the increased import of pickled foreign sheepskins. The major step into manufacture was taken in 1877, when the firm of Messrs Kent and Stevens, tanners and leather dressers of Gloversville, New York, was bankrupted by the fraud of Stevens. Booth's took a mortgage on the factory for debts it was owed.

Manufacture began in a joint venture with John Kent, who died in 1886, when Booth's purchased the factory outright. The initial production was of light finished leathers, particularly gloves.

Chrome tannage, a major technical advance originating in the U.S.A., was developed 1890–1900, Booths was associated with it and the process helped the firm to grow. An efficient method of chemical tanning was of particular value in producing a cheap kid leather (consumption of hides in America 1889–99 increased 21 per cent, sheepskins 39 per cent, but consumption of goatskins increased by 1600 per cent). This development became the speciality of Philadelphia. Also in the late 1890s, the large meat-packing houses began to sell hides cheaply as a by-product, leaving the importing side of Booth's business in serious trouble. Booth's transformation from merchant to manufacturer was thus hastened. Booth's entered an arrangement with a Philadelphia chrome tanner, J. P. Mathieu, who supplied the firm with Brazilian goatskins and received the finished product, marketed as 'Surpass'. Meanwhile, the Gloversville factory was in decline because of the fall in demand for expensive gloves and competition from new Western glove makers. In fact, the Gloversville factory switched to shoe leather. In 1906, the Surpass Leather Company was formed, a majority of shares was held by Booth and Company, with arrangements for the gradual liquidation of the holdings of J. P. Mathieu and Company. Booth's was now a fully integrated manufacturer of leather in the U.S.A.

Alfred Booth and Company expanded from warehouses in New York and Boston; in 1910 the sales network in the South and Mid-West was strengthened by a branch in St Louis, then branches in Cincinnati and Rochester. Salesmen from these centres (equipped with motor cars in 1914) visited local factories. Also of great interest was the growth of an export trade from the U.S.A. to Europe, where chrome tannage was rare. A warehouse was established in Bermondsey, London, and New York agents (Lowenstein and Company) established for Germany and France; later the agents became distributors. Many foreign markets were penetrated, including Russia. The growing volume and profitability of by-products (trimmings of skin used in glue and hair employed in making felt) led to Booth's to acquire interests in the U.S.A. companies of Gardiner-Lucas Glue and Gelatine Corporation and the Densten Felt and Hair Company.

In 1914, Booth's was a widely diversified manufacturer with a growing shipping business, largely dependent on U.S. trade – 27 per cent of the tonnage of the Booth fleet was employed between American ports and half the distance traversed by the ships was in American waters.

Supply difficulties during World War I and difficulties of the shipping line after U.S. entry were followed by 18 months of boom conditions at the end of the war. In the inter-war period, Booth's became an international manufacturer and it is now a supplier and merchant of raw stock. The Surpass Leather Company's factory and the Densten Felt and Hair Company have both been sold.

A further point of interest about Booth's interests in America is that in 1886 the firm was involved in a clash with organised labour. The 'Most Noble Order of the Knights of Labour', powerful at that time in the North-Eastern States, were actively campaigning for higher wages and a 9-hour working day. The Shoeleather Association of Manufacturers rejected these demands and a strike plus demands for the establishment of a co-operative factory (with $25 shares for each participating workman) followed. Charles Booth (Jnr.), later to achieve fame as a social investigator, urged caution and compromise, but his views had little effect from London. The strike collapsed because of the weakness of the Knights of Labour, not from any conciliatory policy adopted by the Shoeleather Association.

Burroughs Wellcome was originally established in the U.K. in 1889 by two Americans. In 1908 they moved to the U.S.A. so to a certain extent this was a repatriation of industry rather than a direct investment. In 1911 a belting factory was set up at Passaic, New Jersey by a U.K. concern called R. & J. Dick. The International Casement Co. of Jamestown, New York, was established in 1912 for the manufacture of metal window frames. Henry Hope was instrumental in this venture with the aid of American capital.

In belting manufacture, a British investment evolved by a tortuous route.[83] In the late nineteenth century two gentlemen of German extraction, Eugene Bartikeit and Charles Treiber, formed a partnership in the U.K. to buy and sell cotton and other goods both at home and abroad. The partnership came to an end and Bartikeit joined W. Willson Cobbett Ltd, where he became Export Director. Treiber emigrated to the U.S.A. in the late 1890s. Up to this point W. Willson Cobbett Ltd had only one or two major business contacts in the U.S.A. In 1902 Treiber formed an agency with George Beach in Boston for the sale of 'Scandinavia' belting imported from the U.K. company. In May 1904 the Scandinavia Belting Co. was formed in Boston as a subsidiary of W. Willson Cobbett Ltd with a fixed nominal capital of $50,000. Beach was appointed treasurer, Bartikeit elected President and Treiber Vice President.

The venture survived a few financial crises in its first couple of years but the orders it generated greatly helped to keep the U.K. mills in full production. Much of the new business resulted from Henry Ford who, in 1908, first ordered vast quantities of narrow, lightly dressed 'MCM' belting, two-foot lengths were used as transmission linings for the epicyclic gear box of Ford Model T cars. The popularity of Model T kept the small looms at Cleckheaton, Yorkshire, fully occupied.

The head office of Scandinavia Belting Co. was re-located in New York and trade continued to flourish in both beltings and Ford linings. In 1911 the name of the U.K. parent was changed to Scandinavia Belting Ltd. In 1912 Beach resigned after disagreement with the people from England and sold his shares to the parent company. Scandinavia Belting Co. thus became a wholly owned subsidiary of Scandinavia Belting Ltd. Mammoth orders for Ford linings continued to be passed on from the wholly owned sales subsidiary until World War I intervened. Manufacturing in the U.S.A. was not started until 1923. In 1925 the name of the parent company was again changed to British Belting and Asbestos Limited, following the acquisition of the British Asbestos Co., and in 1967 to BBA Group Limited.

The Dunlop Pneumatic Tyre Co. Ltd established an American subsidiary in 1869. This was re-incorporated in 1919 as the Dunlop Tire and Rubber Corporation of America. By 1923 the company had fixed assets of $16 million, although before World War I its activities were insignificant.[84] For France, André Michelin had, prior to 1914, all but established a U.S. tyre-producing subsidiary but the scheme was eventually abandoned.[85]

In the soap industry, Lever Brothers (see Chapter 5), which had previously sold its Sunlight soap through U.S. agencies, bought the Curtis Davis Company of Boston in 1897 and the Benjamin Brooke Company of Philadelphia in 1899. Coram estimates that in 1914 Lever's stock of capital in the U.S.A. was $3.75 million.

In the food industry, both Henri Nestlé and Anglo-Swiss Condensed Milk Company (see Chapter 5) operated factories in the U.S.A. but by 1914 only the one belonging to Nestlé remained in Swiss hands. Joseph Tetley set up a subsidiary in tea-packing and merchanting in the U.S.A. in 1913.

Thomas Lipton (born 1850 in Glasgow) went to the U.S.A. at the age of 14 in 1865 and returned to Scotland 4 years later with a wealth of experience of American business conditions.[86] He had been employed in many jobs: labouring on a Virginia tobacco plantation; book-keeping on a South Caroline rice plantation and most importantly, working in a New York grocery store.[87] He saved $500 in the process and began to expand in his own retailing (his father had a small traditional 'corner shop' in Glasgow). This retailing trade was established by finding cheap sources of supply for his U.K. shops, particularly meat, which he imported from Ireland, but even from the beginning he bought low-cost American hams to supplement his main Irish sources. The expansion of his retailing chain was backed by extensive advertising efforts based on American example. Lipton himself said: 'Every business idea, every successful move I have made has been suggested to me by my observation of American methods.'[88] This should be taken with a pinch of salt as he was speaking to an American at the time.

Lipton's next visit to the U.S.A. was to organise a buying agency there (1880).[89] In particular, he wished to purchase bacon and ham since the demand could not be met from Ireland alone. He had already established contracts for the supply of cheese with firms in Upper New York State and for butter in New York and the Mid-West. He claimed that, within a few days of reaching Chicago, he had acquired a hog-packing plant with a capacity of 300–400 hogs per day. The original motive was to supply the U.K. market but, as with Lipton's other ventures, the temptation to achieve growth in as many directions as possible overtook this intention. Mathias[90] suggests that the profit motive combined with the more subtle consideration of giving his managers' enterprise a free rein lay behind this policy. So the Chicago plant, under the title of 'Cork Packing House', began to supply the U.S. domestic market and thus came into competition with the formidable U.S. giants. The U.S. plant provided market intelligence and rising prices as well as its processing commitments. Within 2 years the demands on this plant proved too great and in November 1886 Lipton opened a much larger plant (capacity 2000 hogs per day) in South Omaha, Nebraska.

This was a sudden move to a relatively unknown area. A hotel proprietor and a local merchant had offered to build Lipton's packing-house free of charge if he would start operations on their land and would slaughter every day for a specified number of years. The 'Lipton Packing Company' soon employed 400 people. A New York depot was established and a thriving trade acheived with the West Coast of America. The growing importance of the U.S. market is shown by the development of separate processing techniques and brands: the Johnstone Packing Company for the domestic market and the Lipton Packing Company curing for the U.K. market. However, Nebraska hogs produced a variety of meat too fatty for British tastes and when Armour made an offer of $70,000 for the plant, Lipton found it too advantageous to resist.

Lipton returned to Chicago and purchased the 4½ acre Meyer Packing

House at Union Yards which had a capacity of 2000—4000 hogs per day. He consolidated his meat-packing business around this facility, which was incorporated in 1890. The product-line was diversified from the raw materials into sausages and lard. Lipton invested in a fleet of refrigerated cars in order to develop the West Coast trade, and confined his dealing to the wholesale trade through agents in major cities, with an extensive search for contract trade. The meat-packing business was never brought under the ownership or control of the U.K. parent company. In 1902 Lipton sold the plant to his neighbour in the Union Yards (Armour) for $250,000.

Lipton Ltd was incorporated in the U.K. in 1898 amidst a welter of public euphoria. Incorporation represented 'a financial but not managerial revolution'.[91] Lipton continued to be the sole policy-maker and his position was secure as long as he satisfied his preference-holders and trustees for debentures. Management structure was unchanged and as Lipton's judgement weakened, so problems began to accumulate.

For a few years following 1889, Lipton organised the development of a fully integrated ('from tea garden to tea pot') worldwide tea trade. Lipton's intention was to set up chains of retail shops, including the U.S.A. and Canada, Australia and South Africa. In the first instance, only agency trade was established with one or two retail shops for prestige advertising purposes. After the incorporation of the U.K. company Thomas Lipton's business in North America remained his personal property, connected only as a customer with the rest of Lipton Ltd. The expanding market of the U.S.A. had no tea trade, the minuscule level of demand was met by Chinese and Japanese green tea. Within 2 years of Lipton's visit to Colombo, Ceylon, in 1890, he established a chain of agents in New York and Chicago to push sales in the restaurant and hotel trades. This pilot scheme to test the retail market led to the establishment of four shops to sell tea in the U.S.A. This was short-lived and Lipton decided that the wholesale trade was managerially safer than large-scale shop networks. A continent-wide advertising campaign was introduced to consolidate success and the agency trade flourished. T. J. Lipton Inc. (U.S.A.) and T. J. Lipton Ltd (Canada) were incorporated. Written agreements between these companies and Lipton's in London formally divided their marketing areas — London taking the rest of the world. The North American companies agreed to purchase through Lipton's of London. Sales responded rapidly in the U.S.A. and in August 1919, the East Coast headquarters moved to a large 11-storey building on the waterfront at Hoboken, New Jersey. The Lipton name was emblazoned on the building in large letters to greet ships reaching Manhattan.[92] The North American companies were kept out of the hands of the London company until

1937, after Sir Thomas Lipton's death, when they were sold to a syndicate including Lipton's Ltd and Unilever. In 1946, Unilever bought a controlling interest in Lipton's American business.

Through his career, Thomas Lipton's concern was to create a fully integrated organisation with control over raw materials, intermediate goods, manufacture and distribution, including retailing (although the retailing stage did not fully materialise in the U.S.A.). The internalisation of the complete process gave full control to the entrepreneur as well as security against profit-taking and failure of supplies. The organisational structure was, however, unable to adapt as rapidly as the demands upon it, and managerial deficiencies led to severe problems in the inter-war years.

Waugh attributes Thomas Lipton's particular success in the U.S.A. to the knowledge he gained of the poorer classes on his first visit:

> ... those three years of wandering between the Atlantic Seaboard and the Mississippi were more valuable than any diploma. He saw America as a poor man sees it, which the European who is not an immigrant rarely does. Lipton knew America as Americans themselves know it, by having struggled there. Nor was he ever to mistake Manhattan for America.[93]

In the paint industry, the U.K. firm of International Paints opened a factory at Brooklyn, New York, in 1898. Morgan Crucible was another U.K. firm which operated a subsidiary in the U.S.A. before World War I; it began to manufacture carbon brushes in a factory at Long Island City in 1910. Similarly, British Portland Cement had invested more than $2 million in the Olympic Portland Cement Co. Ltd with properties and factories at Bellingham, Washington, on the Pacific Coast.[94] British Marconi had a £250,000 stake in the Marconi Wireless Telegraph Company of America which was started in 1902; however, this was soon sold to American interests.

Negotiations for the manufacturer of Rolls-Royce engines in the U.S.A. began in May 1917; Claude Johnson, the business brain and entrepreneur behind Rolls-Royce, led them.[95] However, Johnston wanted the U.S. Government to carry much of the financial burden and refused to license production to any U.S. company because he did not wish to pass on any vital proprietary information or to create a competitor. Amalgamation of Rolls-Royce with the U.S. automobile manufacturers Pierce-Arrow was considered, but came to nothing. In 1917, Rolls-Royce of America Inc. was set up to purchase American parts for assembly in the Eagle aero-engine in Derby, England. Johnson acquired a wide knowledge of business conditions in the U.S.A. which were useful in the later establishment of production of motor cars in the U.S.A. In 1917 Johnson commented 'Labour has always been the difficulty of the American Manufacturer — a man can get 10 shillings a day for sweeping the streets of New York'[96] and he foresaw labour supplies as a potential difficulty of producing in the U.S.A. Lloyd concludes: 'Had the decision to mass produce [the Eagle engine] in the United States been taken in 1916, the resulting increase in allied air power towards the latter part of 1917 might well have ended the war a great deal sooner'.[97]

As a result of these experiences and because of the attraction of the U.S.A. for Rolls-Royce — the wealth of the country, the size of the upper income groups, the efficiency of American production methods and the relative freedom from restrictions — Rolls-Royce management decided to produce in the U.S.A. Production was to be strictly controlled from Derby. Parts production began in Springfield, Massachusetts, in July 1920. The production of Rolls-Royce chassis in the U.S.A. was seen as a major form of insurance against political and economic disasters which Johnson feared were about to hamper production at Derby.

Despite avoiding import duties, U.S. production was never totally successful. Springfield Rolls-Royce were subject to product defamation on the grounds that they were not the equal of English-produced Rolls-Royce, although today they are highly regarded by Rolls-Royce cognoscenti. The U.K. management was narrow, dogmatic and inflexible. It totally misjudged the different market requirements of the U.S.A. Production of Rolls-Royce at Springfield ended in 1931.

French companies had small amounts invested in the New York Taxicab Co. Ltd and the Berlitz chain of language schools.[98] Two other firms that opened in the U.S.A. during the war years were S.K.F., the Swedish engineering concern, and the Dutch company, Margarine Uni, later part of Unilever.

The German company Kny-Scherer, established in 1896, was for many years the largest manufacturer and vendor of surgical instruments in the U.S.A. Two other German concerns, De Witt & Hertz and Siemens & Halske (see Chapter 5) also had important places in the industry. In an allied field, foreign interests (De Trey and Company) held one-third interest in the Dentists Supply Company of New York.[99] Finally, F. L. Smidth and Co. A/S of Denmark set up a subsidiary in 1895 to manufacture cement machinery.[100] Some of the above companies are enumerated in Lewis's list (see Table 4.7).

TABLE 4.7 Foreign-owned industrial companies in the U.S.A., 1914 and 1919
(£ thousands unless otherwise stated)

Registration date and company	1914 Capital stock	1914 Funded debt	1919 Capital stock	1919 Funded debt	Notes
1881 Solvay Process	$9,382.3	–	$9,382.3	–	Belgian
1887 Fownes Brothers & Company	$2,676.0	–	$2,678.0	–	
1889 H. H. Warner & Co.	550.0	70.0	550.0	70.0	
Otis Steel	$7,153.7	–	–	–	Bought by Americans in 1919 for $13,000
Pillsbury-Washburn Flour Mills	946.1	1,454.5	946.1	1,353.2	
1895 Semet–Solvay	$2,070.7	–	$2,070.7	–	Belgian
1898 American Thread	$5,400.0	–	$5,400.0	–	
1899 Lever Brothers Co. Ltd	$3,740.0	–	$3,750.0	–	
1908 Dick (R. & J.)	267.3	–	267.3	–	
1910 Massey-Harris Harvester Co. Ltd	$1,687.5	–	$2,062.5	–	Canadian
New York Taxicab Company	$1,683.3	$41.7	$1,683.3	$41.7	French
1911 American Sales Book Co. Ltd	$3,941.0	–	$3,707.0	–	Canadian
Olympic Portland Cement	250.0	121.0	250.0	106.1	
1912 Monarch Knitting Co. Ltd	$500.0	–	$500.0	–	Canadian
1913 Alabama Traction Light & Power Ltd	$17,975.0	$13,452.0	$17,995.0	$25,324.0	Canadian
1916 Riordan Co. Ltd	–	–	$240.0	–	Canadian
TOTAL	$66,288.5	$21,721.2	$59,535.8	$33,012.0	

All companies are British unless otherwise stated.

Source: Lewis (1936), p. 566.

4.18 CONCLUSION

It can be seen from these industry analyses that the over-all spectrum of investment was very large and covered many aspects of U.S. industrial life. However, with few exceptions the investments, particularly the earlier ones, were relatively short-lived and fell into American ownership before long or went out of business altogether. In many of the industries, such as textiles, the British held a dominant position among those European countries investing in the U.S.A. Exceptions to this, however, included the electrical industry where, although the share of the U.S. industry that was foreign-controlled was smaller than that of textiles, it was almost 100 per cent in German hands. The dyestuffs industry was another exception and in that case the foreign-owned sector was 90 per cent in German hands and 10 per cent in Swiss.

Many German direct investments had already struck a modern note by using their U.S. investments as outlets for partly finished goods shipped from Germany. This is early evidence of the international rationalisation of production and of the advent of 'sourcing' policies.

As well as their dyestuffs interest the Swiss had a much larger interest in the food industry, where prior to 1914 they appear to have been the only foreign country with manufacturing interests in the U.S.A. Belgian interest was mainly in the chemical industry and French and Dutch interest in the oil industry, although the former had largely disposed of their interest by the outbreak of World War I.

Probably the only American industry that was very largely foreign-controlled was that of man-made fibres. The American Viscose Corporation, the only firm producing in the U.S.A. at that time, was almost completely owned by Courtaulds in the U.K. This differs from the dyestuffs industry, where although the Germans had 90 per cent of the market it was through exports rather than investment in U.S. industry itself. The problem was that the U.S. industry, rather than being dominated by foreign companies, was simply far too small and consequently the level of imports very high.

Lastly, the U.S. subsidiaries of several European companies can be seen to have dominated the foreign-controlled share of their particular industries. It is this feature of the direct investment that stands out rather than the importance of any particular U.S. industry.[101]

At the level of the individual firm a rich variety of motives for investment has been uncovered. Here we follow a different classification to Brooke and Remmers' (Chapter 1, pp. 5–6).

First, defensive motives were important in a number of industries. Defensive investment came about both to protect a market established by exports from Europe (chemicals, dyes) and in response to projected closure of the U.S. market by tariffs (Solvay in alkalis, Courtaulds in synthetics, Nestlé in foodstuffs, Lever Brothers in soaps). Such defensive motives were reinforced by problems of servicing the U.S. market from a great distance away – transport costs, but also problems of controlling selling, distribution and product servicing. In such cases (dyes, for example), costs were reduced by direct investments. The average cost of production in the U.S.A. fell below marginal costs of production and export in Europe plus transport costs.

A second motive was the desire to control supplies and stocks of raw materials. This vertical integration type of foreign investment characterised much of early direct investment – notably British – but in the U.S.A. was prevalent only in oil and to a small degree in the desire of textile companies to control cotton.

Third, and perhaps most important of all, was the desire of European companies to exploit technological advances through direct investment. This is often the way to secure maximum return from sunk costs in research. Examples span a wide range of industries, pharmaceuticals, metals, electrical industry, synthetic fibres, chemicals and surgical instruments among them.

The need to satisfy local demand effectively was often the motive for investment. Examples here arise in textiles (J. & J. Cash) and in soaps (Lever Brothers). Also, the need to differentiate a product to suit local demand was an influence, e.g. in the automobile industry. Where a local presence is required to keep in touch with demand, foreign investment is necessary.

The influence of international competition was also important, and in attempts to meet competition on a truly world scale (in the oil industry Shell and Standard Oil soon had a global setting) and in desires through the trust system to limit and channel competition which sometimes led to 'co-operative' foreign investments through market sharing/cartel systems. Thus attempts to divide the worldwide market in, for instance, dyes and tobacco, sometimes led to interpenetration of markets, but more often led to restriction on investment.

Finally, we can point to 'induced' foreign investment. Foreign investment in land and cattle companies resulted from spin-offs from railway investments, and in turn, land and cattle companies led to the foreign expansion of mortgages, finance and insurance companies. Banking firms also followed where industrial companies led.

5 Eight Case Histories

5.1 INTRODUCTION

In this chapter the case histories of eight European companies are examined. The companies selected all made direct investments in U.S. manufacturing between 1870 and 1914 and were all prominent among the other European companies investing in the same industry. In some cases, such as Lever Brothers, they were the only foreign investors in their industry. With the exception of the Nobel companies, those selected were all among the first to buy control of, or establish new, genuine subsidiaries. As explained in the case history, the early U.S. Nobel company was autonomous and financially independent but had, in common with other Nobel companies in Europe, an important but minority shareholder in the person of Alfred Nobel himself. The Anglo-Swiss Condensed Milk Company is discussed in the case history with Henri Nestlé because the two companies merged in 1905 and both of their histories before that are relevant to the post-merger situation. Similarly, Siemens and A.E.G. are discussed together because before their separation in 1898 they had many financial and trade links which must be considered.

The companies were also selected to represent a cross-section of European countries. The principal countries in Europe, as far as direct investment in the U.S.A. is concerned, prior to 1914, were the U.K., Germany, Holland, Switzerland and Belgium and, as can be seen in Table 5.1, these are all represented in the case histories.

In the concluding sections of the case histories, the reasons for the success or failure of the ventures are identified and examined. In addition, where relevant, a comparison is drawn between the U.S. venture and any other foreign direct investments that the companies made at around the same time. In the case of Courtaulds the U.S. venture was its only overseas investment prior to 1914.

TABLE 5.1 Countries of origin of the companies selected

Case history number	Company	Country of origin
1	Lever Brothers	U.K.
2	Courtaulds	U.K.
3	Royal Dutch Shell	U.K. and Holland
4	Nobel and Nobel Explosives Trust Co.	Sweden, U.K. and Germany
5	Fiat	Italy
6	Solvay	Belgium
7	Nestlé and Anglo-Swiss Condensed Milk Co.	Switzerland
8	Siemens and A.E.G.	Germany

5.2 LEVER BROTHERS (U.K.)[1]

In 1897, Lever Brothers of Port Sunlight, which was then the largest U.K. soap manufacturer, bought a controlling interest in the American firm of Curtis Davis and Company of Cambridge, Massachussetts. Lever Brothers outlined three reasons for entering the U.S. market or indeed any other foreign market.

(1) Tariffs, particularly in the U.S.A., had over the last 25 years or so become more and more of a problem to its export business. (The U.S. *ad valorem* duty in the 1890s, except for a short period at 10 per cent, was 20 per cent.)
(2) Differing local tastes in overseas markets could best be both diagnosed and catered for by production in the particular country or region.
(3) Lever's business in the U.S.A. had reached the size where it justified its own support production locally and no longer production in England and export to the U.S.A.

This last reason was Lever's principal criterion in the foreign investment decision process and because of the problem of control from Port Sunlight, he liked to maintain each overseas unit as a separate limited company.

Lever Brothers' connection with the U.S.A. began in 1888 when William H. Lever (later the First Viscount Leverhulme) visited the country to study U.S. selling methods and to arrange agency representation for soaps then made in the U.K. In 1892 land was acquired in Toronto to establish the first Canadian works, and the first U.S. agency began operation. In 1890 Lever purchased a run-down cottonseed oil mill at Vicksburg, Mississippi, which he converted to a profitable business. This mill carried on operations for 10 years and was sold when larger-scale oil mills were established at Port Sunlight, U.K. In March 1895 the New York branch sales office opened. Lever wrote from the U.S. to his father in 1895 of his U.S. undertaking: 'It is the biggest undertaking I ever had on hand and I fancy it has depressed me.'

In 1895 the market for soap in the U.S.A. was highly competitive, which may account for the initial (unusual) trepidation. Sunlight soap was a pure yellow laundry bar and faced stiff competition from larger and less pure domestic yellow bars at lower prices.

At an early stage, a critical mistake was made in marketing methods. Contacts with jobbers (wholesale merchants) were not cultivated – Lever Brothers preferred to rely on their own salesmen and it was not until 1912 that Lever Brothers became closely linked with jobbers, a policy which paid off, particularly in recessions, when jobbers' loyalty helped to move stock. In the early years, jobbers boycotted Lever Brothers' goods and the firm carried a large number of retailers on its 'direct' list.

Before 1897 all Lever Brothers' U.K. exports were therefore handled by the branch office in New York established in 1895, and this was apparently still quite small when the Massachusetts company was purchased. This branch had been selling Lifebuoy and Sunlight soap manufactured in the U.K. In the first year of operation the branch sold 374 cases of Lifebuoy and 48,000 cases of Sunlight. Lever took three-fifths of the capital of Curtis Davis and the rights to the established 'Welcome' brand soap, which was later to prove a valuable asset. In 1898 the manufacture of Sunlight and Lifebuoy began in Cambridge; the entire business was transferred there in 1899 when the remaining U.S. interests were purchased. The need for local manufacture had been established and the new company became Lever Brothers Ltd (Boston Works), founded with a private capital of $1.5 million.

Lever Brothers bought their second U.S. company, Benjamin Brooke Company of Philadelphia, in 1899. The object here was to use Brooke's to cover all the U.S. sales outside the New England states, which was the responsibility of the Massachusetts company. The 1900 sales were: 5318 cases Lifebuoy, 67,399 Welcome (a tallow soap), 51,287 cases Sunlight (an oil soap), and 20,044 cases of Monkey brand scouring soap – a brand acquired by the takeover of Brooke's. In 1903 the name Lever Brothers Company was adopted.

In 1900, Lever Brothers had a total of five overseas companies. All were small by Port Sunlight standards and the one in Philadelphia was the smallest. By 1906, in spite of new factory teething troubles, most of Lever Brothers Company's overseas operations were making profits and these were almost invariably ploughed back for expansion. At that time the capital tied up overseas was at £1 million, over 25 per cent of the total Lever Brothers capital.

The Americans retained a minority interest for some time in the Philadelphia plant, but Lever Brothers Company's two U.S. investments were consolidated into one after a few years and at that time the British firm bought out all the remaining American interest. Lever Brothers Company's two established U.K. products, Sunlight and Lifebuoy were, prior to 1914, never very successful and in addition, the company always faced stiff local competition wherever it went. On a more national basis, there were several serious competitors: Procter & Gamble, Colgate, Fel and a collection of meat-packing concerns such as Armour, Swift and Cadahy. These companies made soap as a sideline of their main business and, in addition to being much larger concerns than Lever was in the U.S.A., they also controlled one of the world's principal supplies of tallow. Even after the invention of the hydrogenation process had reduced the importance of tallow, they still represented a major problem to William Lever and he was unable to come to any agreements with them to reduce the problem until after 1914.

In 1909, Lamont, Corliss & Company were appointed exclusive agents for the 'General Territory' (the company divided the U.S.A. into New England and 'General Territory'). Lamont, Corliss had headquarters in New York with branch sales offices in Philadelphia, Chicago and other key cities – the hope was to give better services to retailers and jobbers. New England was used as a testing ground for new marketing methods, applied, if successful, in the General Territory. New methods of helping the dealer to market his goods were devised.

By 1912 sales of Sunlight soap had fallen to only one-third of those in 1901, Lever Brothers Company's best year. This was mainly because the American housewives preferred the larger 'filled' American bars of soap to the small, although just as effective, tablets of Sunlight. By the same time, Lifebuoy sales had struggled to three times their 1901 figure and the Welcome brand it had purchased was fairly successful. Lifebuoy sales were mainly outside the New England states.

A critical development occurred in late 1912 when Francis A. Countway was appointed general manager of the U.S. operation. Countway had started his career at Lever Brothers in 1896 as a bookkeeper, with a promise of the first sales job that became available. He became the most successful salesman (it seems by the simple expedient of working harder and longer than the rest) and he instituted the company's first real advertising and sales promotion campaigns. In 1915 a $44,000 expansion of plant took place and sales passed 250,000 cases. In 1916 the first real advertising effort was put behind Lux flakes and in 3 years its sales multiplied by 10. Its success was due to the rapid development in the market for silks and fine fabrics in women's fashions, which led to an increasing demand for a product which would clean these more fragile fabrics. The 100,000 cases of Lux flakes sold in 1915 became over 1 million by 1918.

Further product innovations backed by advertising took place. In 1919 Rinso, the first granulated laundry soap, was launched. With the contemporary introduction of the washing machine, Rinso (its introduction delayed for 2 years by the effects of World War I), established immediate brand leadership as the 'soap in granules for the family wash'. Old products were dropped (Sunlight was allowed to die in 1912) so that Levers could concentrate on winners.

Countway also steered the company through a massive 50 per cent increase in raw materials costs in 1915. He was in a fortunate position to be well covered. He also tried to keep to a policy of price stability (also when the price fell) to maintain consumer loyalty.

In the years 1918–19 a new selling policy was adopted, replacing middlemen with an exclusively Lever sales force. Such reorganisation and development was justified by the vast increases in the sales volume of Lux, the secure position of Lifebuoy and the introduction of Rinso. Sales offices were established first in New York, then Philadelphia, Chicago, San Francisco and Kansas City. Thus a countrywide sales force was gradually built up. The growth of employment is shown in Table 5.2.

In 1914 Lever signed an agreement with Procter & Gamble which led to the formation of the Hydrogenation Company. This was established to control the patents of both parties and from Lever's point of view helped to safeguard their future in the U.S.A.

The period 1897–1914, although not actually a disaster for Lever Brothers as far as the U.S.A. was concerned, was singularly unsuccessful. Profits throughout the period were minimal: out of total sales of $800,000 in 1913, profits only amounted to $733.[2] This early investment did, however, establish Lever Brothers' brand names in the U.S.A. and laid the foundation for what was to become a highly successful operation after World War I. In the years that followed the initial U.S. acquisition, the existence of his U.S. subsidiary helped Lever to test some products at a stage when their cost made them prohibitive anywhere except the U.S.

TABLE 5.2 Lever Brothers Company employees: Cambridge office and factory (year closing day)

Year	Number of employees	Total number of employees including division offices and 'Field'
1902	110	110
1903	199	199
1904	147	147
1905	108	108
1907	145	145
1908	118	118
1909	125	125
1910	126	126
1911	119	119
1912	145	145
1913	156	156
1914	148	148
World War I		
1919	979	1,058*
1929	1897	2,180*

* Approximate
Source: Author's research at Unilever House — Company papers.

market. In addition, many of Lever's ideas on marketing and technology, and more especially advertising, were by-products of his observations while in the U.S.A.[3] In 1922 the then Lord Leverhulme said: 'We get enormous strength on the selling side in England by our knowledge of selling and advertising in overseas companies, especially in the United States'.[4]

Although tariffs and sales volume were important criteria in Lever Brothers' foreign investment decision process, a large part was due to William Lever's personal fascination with the U.S.A. It can be seen, therefore, that although Lever's decision to invest in the U.S.A. may have been motivated by factors other than commercial ones and as a result, the investment may have yielded an extremely poor return, it was not altogether wasted. At the same time, it is possible to identify several factors that probably contributed to the poor return.

Wilson maintains that one factor was that increasing U.S. tariffs were changing the character of British capital exports from portfolio to direct investment and that Lever was a pioneer of direct investment in U.S. commercial enterprise and industrial manufacturing. He states, '... Lever was in the van but he had to pay the penalty of the pioneer whose privilege it is to let others profit by his experience'.[5] Although this was undoubtedly true, other direct investors just as much in the vanguard as Lever, did succeed in making satisfactory returns on their investment, indeed Courtaulds' return was so satisfactory that it became an embarrassment to the company. Faith points out other factors which were presumably more to blame for the lack of profits than the pioneer theory. He states, '... Lever's ventures in the U.S. before the 1914—18 war were a classic lesson in the futility, not of me-tooism, but of trying to introduce purely foreign products into an alien market'.[6] In other words, although Sunlight and Lifebuoy were winners in the U.K. and although they had been exported to the U.S.A. in considerable volume, they were not in accord with American taste and consequently were unsuccessful. A second factor Faith identifies is that Lever would not use middlemen (as Procter & Gamble did), so he was virtually confined to the New England market where he sold directly to retailers. Again, the method of selling in the U.K., although successful there, was not correct for the U.S. market. Lever learned these lessons the hard way, but it took until World War I to do so and not until after the war did the U.S. venture begin to pay. During the unprofitable period, the American operation was largely subsidised by the other overseas ventures which performed much better. New overseas factories that Lever established in the period 1898—1913 are set out in Table 5.3.

TABLE 5.3 Lever Brothers' new overseas factories established between 1898 and 1913

Date	Location	Reason for investment
1898	Olten, Switzerland	Sales volume justified local production
1900	Toronto, Canada	Sales volume justified local production
1900	Mannheim, Germany	Sales volume justified local production
1900	Balmain, Australia	Avoidance of local tariffs
1901 (Begun but not opened until 1915)	Vlaardingen, Holland	Sales volume justified local production
1904	Brussels, Belgium	Sales volume justified local production
1908	Vienna, Austria	Packaging operation only, to avoid tariffs
1910	Lille, France	Sales volume justified local production
1910	Gothenburg, Sweden	Sales volume justified local production
1910	Oslo, Norway	Sales volume justified local production
1913	Tori Shindon, Japan (between Kobe and Osaka)	Sales volume justified local production

Source: Wilson (1954), and author's research.

In addition to these new factories, Lever bought a stake in three European soap companies as he had done in the two American ones. In 1910 he bought a half interest in Dr Thompson's Seifenpulver which had factories at Wittenburg and Dusseldorf in Germany, and in 1913 to help cover the parts of France not readily serviceable from Lille, he bought control of two small factories in Marseilles.

None of these were without teething trouble but, apart from the Austrian venture which was never a success, they were ultimately profitable and helped to offset the American performance. Lever had, of course, many other overseas operations prior to 1914, but these were all connected with the supply of raw materials and not manufacturing.

Lever's U.S. investment was a disappointment only in financial terms. In terms of the experience gained in marketing which was later put to good use in the U.K. and elsewhere, it must be regarded as a success.

It has been said that the history of Lever Brothers is a history of its advertising. In the U.S.A. at least, this is only partly true. Lever's U.S. success dates from its first successful promotion in 1916 under Countway and the 'Health' campaign following the 1918 influenza epidemic boosted Lifebuoy sales from 211,000 cases (1917) to 331,000 in 1918 (Lever's first advertising manager, Arthur F. Bernhard, was appointed in 1918). It is more instructive to look at marketing policy as a whole. Of crucial importance appears to be the choice of distribution channels. For a new company entering a highly competitive market, to attempt to dispense with middlemen (jobbers) was an act of folly, not only of arrogance. This mistake was not corrected until 1912, when a firm link with jobbers was cemented. The decision to internalise nationwide marketing by creating a wholly owned sales force was a logical one when inroads had been made and where the company had in its possession brand leaders and innovative products. This sales force was backed by extensive advertising and rewards on repeat buying for retailers and consumers alike.

The selling efficiency of Bernhard and experience in sales planning and the management of a sales team in the field was to prove a major strength in the years immediately before and after World War I. Consumer loyalty was retained by 'give-aways'. It was these skills rather than the more gimmicky merchandising contests (started in 1929 in the U.S.A. – 30 years previously in the U.K.) and house-to-house sales (also started first in the U.K.), which were transferable and gave Levers worldwide strength in later years. By 1929, Lever Brothers Company was the third largest manufacturer of soap and glycerine in the U.S.A. In 1930 a plant at Hammond, Indiana, then the most modern plant in the world, was opened.

Levers entered the food market in 1932; in 1937 the firm acquired Lipton's Tea, and in 1944 the Pepsodent Company. All were backed by a huge marketing effort.

5.3 COURTAULDS LTD (U.K.)[7]

Courtaulds' first transaction in the U.S.A. was in August 1908 when it signed an agreement with Silas W. Pettit who ran the Genasco Silk Works and held the American patents for the new viscose or artificial silk manufacturing process. Pettit himself had not had a great deal of success with the process up to that time. The agreement allowed Courtaulds to export its new synthetic products from the U.K. to the U.S.A. on payment of 3 cents per pound to Pettit. This was a lucrative deal for Pettit but he did not gain from it personally: he died 3 months later and was succeeded by his son.

The arrangement continued for some time, but in May 1909 as a result of new Payne–Aldrich tariffs, a new duty was levied on Courtaulds' exports. This duty was set at 45 cents per pound minimum or 30 per cent *ad valorem*, whichever was higher. This made it imperative that Courtaulds establish production facilities behind the tariff wall. Courtaulds knew other European producers were thinking along similar lines so in June 1909, after extensive negotiations, the firm paid Pettit Jnr. $150,000 or £31,000 (the 1909 equivalent) for all his U.S. patents. This move by Courtaulds was as successful as the one 5 years before when they bought their own original patents for £25,000.

In November 1909, considering the notorious U.S. labour shortage, a site was purchased for $50,000 at Marcus Hook near Chester, Pennsylvania. Because of state laws concerning the restrictions on foreign corporations owning and running U.S. companies, the American Viscose Company was formed in February 1910. Courtaulds held virtually all the shares, but to comply with the law they appointed various 'dummy' directors for the new company which in turn leased the land from a specially formed trust. The capital of the new company was fixed at $1 million. The plant was equipped with machines from France and spinning frames from England and became operational early in 1911. It was successful from the very start and Courtaulds' main problem became one of appearing to be earning lower profits than it was.

In 1913, action was proposed in the U.S.A. to reduce the tariff on imports of viscose to increase competition. This came about for two reasons: Courtaulds' involvement with the French in a European viscose cartel; and the fact that the only American producer of Viscose was virtually wholly owned by a foreign corporation.

Successful lobbying by the American Viscose Company and its influential friends eventually won the day. The tariff reduction was not implemented and 1913 was the company's best year to date. The threat did, however, instigate a period of manipulation of the American plant's capitalisation in an attempt to make the profits look more reasonable. Before December 1913 the company had effectively been paying Courtaulds a royalty for the use of their U.S. patents but at this point its capital was increased to $2 million and the company bought the patents for a 4-year period and a reduced royalty payment was agreed. Lustre Fibres, another Courtaulds sales subsidiary already established in New York, was then used to channel all the American company's sales through, as had been happening for some time with Courtaulds' exports to the U.S.A. In spite of these measures, however, the American Viscose Company's net return on its subscribed capital, although falling from 77.8 per cent in 1912 to 36.5 per cent in 1916, rose to 82.6 per cent in 1914. This necessitated further steps.

In May 1915 the Viscose Company with a capital of $10 million was set up to buy the original company. Courtaulds again held nearly all the shares but this time the new company agreed to buy outright Courtaulds' U.S. patents for $5 million, to be paid with interest over 10 years. Even this measure failed to achieve all it was intended to, and the continued profitability of its American subsidiary was to remian an embarrassment to Courtaulds for some time.

Courtaulds' American subsidiary was, prior to 1914, their only overseas investment and was undeniably a tremendous success. This was due largely to the two inspired purchases of the patents for the manufacture of rayon, first in the U.K. and then in the U.S.A. In addition, Courtaulds' U.K. experience was used to the best advantage in the U.S.A. If there was a failure, it was the inability of the company, in spite of several financial manipulations, to avoid making what would have appeared to the Americans as an excessive return on their investment. This factor more than any other kept the subsidiary in the public eye and made it impossible for the Americans to forget that their only source of rayon was U.K.-controlled. It is unfair, however, to label this problem as a failure because by any other yardstick, such as profitability, rate of growth, or return on investment, Courtaulds' U.S. investment must rank as one of the most successful of all the European ventures in the U.S.A. at that time. It was certainly one of the very few, if not the only one, to become notorious because of its profit levels.

5.4 ROYAL DUTCH SHELL (HOLLAND/U.K.)[8]

The Shell Transport and Trading Company was formed in 1897 to take over and consolidate the many activities of the Samuel family. Marcus Samuel started a shop in the East End of London in 1833 to sell antiques and bric-a-brac, including oriental shells. The trade in shells became profitable, so he began to organise direct shipments from the Far East. This developed into a general import and export business and in 1878 his son (also Marcus Samuel), took over the business and added cased kerosene to his general import business. In 1890, the first tankers were ordered to transport oil and in 1892 the first one made its maiden voyage through the Suez Canal. Bulk oil storage points were established in the Far East. The company prospered and, ironically, as it turned out later, rejected a takeover bid from John D. Rockefeller's Standard Oil Company in 1895. A few not so prosperous years followed until 1901 when the situation was radically changed following a deal between Marcus Samuel and the Mellon's Company in the U.S.A., which later became Gulf. The deal was the supply, at a fixed price, of 100,000 tons of oil each year for 21 years from the giant Texas Spindletop fields which the Mellons had just discovered — Samuel was to use this source to supply many parts of Europe, including the U.K. Standard Oil again approached Shell with a takeover offer later in the same year and this time the offer was worth £8 million if Standard Oil got complete control.

Meanwhile in Holland, Henri Deterding who had joined the Royal Dutch Company in 1896 was watching the Standard–Shell negotiations with not a little concern — the firm also had considerable oil interests. (The firm was founded in 1890 to look for oil in the Dutch East Indies.) Deterding could see that such a link-up could spell disaster for his company, and in fact, before the Standard–Shell talks were complete Deterding had made it clear to Samuel how much more successful it would be for Shell if they were to join with Royal Dutch. In 1897 Royal Dutch had prevented Standard buying up their stock at a depressed price by creating a new preference share available only to citizens of the Netherlands. Eventually Samuel turned down Standard's offer leaving the way clear for some sort of agreement with Deterding. In 1902, with Rothschilds of France as a third partner, an agreement was arrived at to form a subsidiary company called the Asiatic Petroleum Company to be registered in the U.K. The idea was that the company would control and administer all the mutual interests of the three parties, but in the event this did not occur, although Asiatic began business in 1903. However, by 1900 Shell and Royal Dutch had both become completely vertically integrated oil companies, with their own transport and refining facilities as well as access to crude oil.

In the meantime, however, Samuel had become preoccupied with his role as Lord Mayor of London (it had been his lifelong ambition to be London's first Jewish Lord Mayor) and this led to another deterioration in Shell's position. In 1906 Samuel found himself in the position of having no alternative but to accept a full merger with Royal Dutch on terms that gave Deterding the upper hand. In 1907, therefore, two of the largest companies in Europe joined as Royal Dutch Shell with the distribution of stock 60 to 40 in favour of the Dutch. In fact, three companies, one U.K., one Dutch and one Asiatic, were formed. Royal Dutch were at that time drawing oil from Russia, Eastern Europe and the Dutch East Indies (later to become Indonesia). The merger took place at a critical time when people in Europe and the U.S.A. were just becoming owners of cars in real quantity. As a result, the demand for oil in the U.S.A. and Europe began to rise dramatically.

Deterding had quickly recognised that the U.S.A. represented by far the largest single market available to him, and because he was increasingly coming up against Americans in all his other operations around the world, particularly in the Far East which was his own major sphere of interest, he decided to commence operations in the U.S.A. Standard's policy of price-cutting, which led to the Europeans merging, also led them to attack Standard's home market to prevent monopoly pricing giving Standard an internationally transmittable advantage.

The history of the company in the U.S.A. begins in 1904 with the first oil cargo Deterding sold there – ironically, this cargo was diverted to Philadelphia from Germany when Standard cut prices in Germany. The years 1910 and 1911 saw a series of price wars in Europe and Asia and the decision was made that an assault must be made on the U.S. market. At this time Deterding attempted to form an alliance with the minor U.S. companies to fight Standard but it failed – his negotiations with the president of the Indian Refining Company of Illinois came to nothing.

In January 1911 two Shell agents arrived in the U.S.A. to organise marketing activities, particularly on the West Coast since this was closest to Shell's refineries in Sumatra. In May 1911 the Supreme Court decided that the Standard Oil Trust (created by John D. Rockefeller), constituted an illegal combine under the 1889 Sherman Act and it was ordered to be broken down into 33 separate organisations. In fact, this did not have a great impact on Shell because the European company had already decided to enter the market, and at the time the company felt that the order was a 'legal trick' and that the Standard companies would, in any case, act in concert (there is some evidence that this occurred for at least a decade).

Shell's first U.S. company, American Gasoline Company, was incorporated in New York in September 1912 to own and operate Pacific Coast marketing properties (the name Shell had been pre-empted by a local firm) after six small oil-producing companies had been purchased in Oklahoma earlier in the year. The company's first ocean terminal was opened at Richmond Beach, Washington, where the first cargo of 'good Sumatra gasoline' was unloaded in September 1912. Five depots were organised with local agents doing the selling on a commission basis. In October 1912 the second U.S. company, Roxana Petroleum Company of Oklahoma, was organised to control the oil-producing facilities, so Shell entered the market from the crude oil end here as opposed to its marketing entry on the West Coast.

However, despite the high quality of Sumatra oil, and prices below Standard's, Deterding decided to buy local producing properties in California (local oil was currently — 1913 — being stored as prices were depressed). Consequently, in August 1913 Shell purchased California Oilfields Ltd for $13 million from the U.K. firm of Balfour, Williamson Company, who had managed the company for 10 years. The properties at Coalinga, California, were one of the largest in that state, producing 4.4 million barrels of oil annually.

Soon afterwards, Shell began to move downstream by setting up as its own retailer, and careful management ensured that independent owners did not feel threatened. Shell also absorbed several small firms such as Seaboard Oil Company (blending and grease firm), thus acquiring established brand names. Also in 1915, the Trumble refining company was purchased for $1 million cash to acquire (and improve on) refining patents. Shell was therefore able to include this technology in what has been described as the first modern refinery at Martinez on the San Francisco Bay. To link it with the oilfields a 170-mile pipeline was begun in October 1914 and the Valley Pipe Line Company organised to build it. The line was completed in August 1915 and the first unit of the refinery began operation in December of that year; initial capacity was 5500 barrels per day, increasing to 18,000 per day by 1918. With this refinery Shell began producing the full range of oil-based products, thus expanding from gasoline only.

Later in 1914 Shell put out a contract for three 8500-ton tankers to fly the U.S. flag. Although this ran into a range of legal difficulties the war resolved the problem — two tankers were operated by the group under charter and one was taken over by the U.S. navy. In July 1914 the American Gasoline Company became Shell Company of California Inc. and in July 1915, a new Shell Company of California was chartered under the laws of California (the New York company was dissolved in 1916).

Meanwhile, in Oklahoma the Roxana company was developing. It was welcomed by the independent oil companies, not only because of its competition to Standard, but also as a prospective customer for the producing properties. The company did have difficulty initially in purchasing producers because of the necessity for approval from London. An attempt was made to buy Gulf Oil from the Mellon family, but it failed. Eventually, the Yarhola leases (Cushing, Oklahoma) were purchased in May 1915, which brought with it a 25-mile pipeline (bought at a time of overproduction). In September 1915 extensive leases in Healdton, Oklahoma were bought, mainly from British entrepreneurs, and the capitalisation of the company was increased from $1 to $5 million. This purchase meant that in the years 1916—18 Shell controlled more than 4 per cent of U.S. crude oil production. As a war measure, refining installations were set up at Cushing and closed in 1919. In 1918 a permanent refinery near St Louis was established, connected by a 428-mile pipeline to Cushing. The push for full integration of production, transport, refining and selling in the Mid-continental region of the U.S.A. was thus almost complete by the end of World War I.

The end of this period saw the Shell companies striving for full integration after entering through marketing on the Pacific Coast and crude oil production in Oklahoma. Later periods of failure to find oil in the U.S.A. and the unfortunate sale of a (later) highly successful well led to the Roxana company's reputation of being 'jinxed'. Later successful exploration eliminated this reputation.

An interesting sideline on Royal Dutch Shell's early U.S. activities is the innovations in employee welfare which the company introduced. In 1917 Roxana introduced the Provident Fund (an import from Holland, where it was established in 1912). A 10 per cent personal salary payment into the fund by an employee was matched by the company as a lump sum retirement or resignation payment, occasionally with an added bonus.

TABLE 5.4 Data on Shell's activities in the U.S.A., 1912–20

	Sales ($)			Net income ($)					Net crude oil production (thousands of barrels)		
	Total	Shell Pacific Coast	Shell Mid-Continent	Total	Shell Pacific Coast	Shell Mid-Continent	Shell Pipeline Cos.		Total	Shell Pacific Coast	Roxana
1912	398,200	48,935	349,265	133,265	(11,000)	144,265			443	–	443
1913	1,334,481	465,714	868,767	220,730	(26,983)	261,687			723	–	723
1914	1,782,047	1,383,103	398,944	140,289	57,000	88,669			505	4,628*	505
1915	2,863,977	1,723,000	1,140,977	536,543	38,000	502,706	(3,941)		5,704	3,104	2,600
1916	11,254,607	7,180,907	4,073,700	2,430,600	580,000	1,849,077	1,536		8,836	4,752	4,884
1917	16,475,919	9,832,063	6,643,856	866,162	589,000	126,365	150,797		9,279	6,293	2,986
1918	23,442,196	14,567,175	8,875,021	2,274,096	1,689,000	875,455	(290,359)		9,503	6,788	2,715
1919	23,744,573	14,509,962	9,234,611	4,384,137	3,344,000	1,146,711	(106,574)		9,157	6,695	2,462
1920	38,687,400	22,186,380	16,501,020	8,830,872	5,891,000	2,454,745	485,127		9,211	6,145	3,065

( ) Indicates losses; * includes last 4 months of 1913.

Source: Kendall Beaton (1951), pp. 782, 783, 784.

Shell of California followed this in 1915. However, an attempt to apply this fund to all employees, not just staff, failed, and it was not successful until a quarter of a century later. A company magazine was started in January 1918, particularly for employees who had been involved in the war, but it was discontinued in December 1920. Shell also gave encouragement and assistance to volunteers for the U.S. war effort and gave an assurance of a job on return. During the war payments were made to families of volunteer employees and payments into the Provident Fund were continued by the company. The company was unusually generous for the era and forward-looking in personnel relations.

Shell's entry into the U.S.A. came at the opposite ends of the spectrum of the vertically integrated oil business. In California the original intention was to market the imported gasoline on the Pacific Coast, then crude sources were acquired and integration required a pipeline and refinery so attention was directed back to crude supplies. In Oklahoma control of crude oil gave the impetus to forward integration. Both chances were seized.

The success of Shell was due to the dramatic upsurge in demand for gasoline derived from the expansion in demand for automobiles. In 1895, 300 cars were sold in the U.S.A., 78,000 in 1905, 459,000 in 1910 and 1,700,000 in 1914. Demand on this scale was largely unforeseen.

The story has a curiously modern note to it in that the oil industry saw very early in the century the development of worldwide competition between large companies. The battle of Royal Dutch Shell and Standard Oil were very quickly worldwide. This early establishment of an oligopolistic market structure led to tactics which are far more familiar today — rivals attempting to match each other in worldwide markets so that the advantages of monopoly control in one area cannot disturb the competitive balance in another — examples are price and advertising wars and the desire for a vertical structure to link markets to raw materials. The Shell story is one of pioneering, not only in early entry to the U.S. market but in developing a worldwide competitive strategy. Table 5.4 shows how Shell's activities developed in the U.S.A. from 1912 to 1920.

5.5 NOBEL AND THE NOBEL EXPLOSIVES TRUST COMPANY (SWEDEN/U.K./GERMANY)[9]

Alfred Nobel, who was born in Sweden in 1833, worked there for many years trying to produce a safe explosive and an equally safe device for setting it off. He eventually achieved this in the form of dynamite which he then proceeded to exploit around the world. In 1871, after many years of being frustrated by the British government in his attempts to start a factory in England, he started production at Ardeer on the west coast of Scotland. This was one of a group of companies founded in various countries with the help of local finance and in which Nobel had shares but no overall control.

The Scottish plant had about £24,000 of capital of which Nobel provided half and a group of prominent Scots including Charles Tennant provided the rest. Tennant was already operating a substantial chemical plant in Glasgow and he and Nobel recognised that at that time the U.K. represented the largest market in the world for explosives and that manufacture there was essential to avoid transport costs. The Scottish company was called the British Dynamite Company.

In 1865, six years before the Scottish investment, Nobel established the Alfred Nobel Company in Hamburg (which was then in Prussia), and this later became the Dynamit–Aktiengesellschaft. In 1866, he founded the U.S. Blasting Oil Company in New York as well as the Giant Powder Company of San Francisco and the Atlantic Giant Powder Company. These latter two companies were founded to cover the areas of the U.S.A. that the New York plant could not reach, and both were operational by 1868. Nobel never actually returned to the U.S.A. after 1868 and he soon discovered that he could not deal with the U.S. investments at long range. It was not surprising that he began to dispose of his American interests and the last of these were finally sold in 1885.

In 1887 the British Dynamite Company merged with the Westquarter Chemical Company. This was another company in which Nobel had acquired a substantial stake and the new combine, called the Nobel's Explosive Company Ltd, had a starting capital of £240,000.

In 1881 the English patents on dynamite ran out and with the increasing competition from home and abroad, and often from other Nobel factories which were in direct competition, something had to be done. The German explosives industry was at that time becoming increasingly dominant in world explosive trade, and in 1884 the German companies signed a price-fixing agreement which was followed by an amalgamation of the four largest in 1885. In 1886 the famous Nobel Dynamite Trust Company was registered. This was a combine of the German trust and Nobel's Explosives of Glasgow and because Nobel's was the largest of the subsidiaries, the new trust was registered in the U.K. It was to remain operational until 1915 when as a result of World War I it was dismembered into its British and German components.

The Nobel Dynamite Trust Co. was to have two attempts at investment in the U.S.A. In 1886, immediately after its foundation, the trust, through Nobel's Explosives of Glasgow, took up 59 per cent of the $100,000 capital of the Standard Explosive Company of New York. This was a new company being formed at Tom's River, New Jersey, to challenge American explosive manufacturers including DuPont. In 1888, however, the Nobel Dynamite Trust Co. sold its shares after threats from the American producers that they would start up in Europe if it did not. As part of the deal the so-called 'American Convention' was signed which was in effect a large-scale, market-sharing and price-fixing agreement between the U.S. and European producers.

The second attempt to enter the U.S.A. was made in 1897. The trust, through an alliance made with the German Powder Group in 1889, attempted to establish a U.S. plant. Again there was a dramatic threat of retaliation by the U.S. producers (chiefly DuPont) and the trust withdrew. Coincidentally, a new 10-year market-sharing agreement was signed by the various parties in October that year.

The story of the Nobel involvement in the U.S.A. falls into two parts both of which failed but for different reasons. Nobel himself was a brilliant inventor but his flair for business was less than brilliant. He relied on his partners in his joint venture for their profitable operation and suffered himself because he never held a controlling interest in the companies so that they all operated autonomously. The only common link between them was that in each case Nobel himself was a minority shareholder. This situation was satisfactory until the tremendous competition from around the world due to the general surplus of supply over demand began to erode profit margins. The competition was such that Nobel's own plants frequently bid against each other, and when the German trust was formed as a result of competition within Germany the situation became intolerable and led to the amalgamation of the U.K. plant with the German trust. The American company did not fail as such but Nobel, because of his reluctance to return to the U.S.A. after its foundation period and his preoccupation with the other plants in Europe and elsewhere, was not able to hold on to the stake that he had in it. The problem was really one of Nobel's inability to look after and protect his own minority interest in the company.

The second part of the story of the Nobel involvement in the U.S.A. was the two attempts of the Nobel Dynamite Trust Co. to buy its way into the U.S. explosives industry. In both cases they could successfully have done so but withdrew at the last minute because of American threats to retaliate in Europe. These were classic examples of the cartels on a global scale which existed at the turn of the century. In the case of the Nobel Trust, it was felt that they could not afford to risk the intervention of the Americans into the European market which at that time they had to themselves.

The Nobel involvements in the U.S.A. were never a success as foreign investments, although the companies that Nobel himself founded but later withdrew from completely, did survive under American ownership.

5.6 FIAT (ITALY)[10]

Almost from its beginning the Fiat company was an important exporter, and in the early days the name Fiat became synonymous, in the importing countries, with luxury, large-engined and expensive cars. By 1903, Fiat was exporting sizeable quantities of its cars to the U.S. market because they were so suitable. A successful period for Fiat then followed when the cars performed well in racing. This success further stimulated their U.S. sales and by 1907 they were second in the imported car league (see Table 5.5).

The firm of Hollander and Tangeman were responsible for all Fiat's exports to the U.S.A. They sold and serviced Fiats and, in a small way, put American bodies on imported chassis. This business flourished and in 1908 the firm opened a big new repair depot in New York. Later that year the largest-ever single shipment of cars arrived in the U.S.A. from Europe. It comprised 31 cars — all from Fiat.

By 1910 American buyers of Fiat cars had a choice of five models and in that year sales in the U.S.A. first warranted a U.S. production unit. This was established largely by American capital at Poughkeepsie, New York, to make Fiats under licence from Italy. Fiat of Italy did, however, have a stake in the company and were able to exercise a significant level of

TABLE 5.5 Number of European cars imported into the U.S.A. in 1907

Maker	Number imported
Renault	266
Fiat	181
Mercedes	94
Panhard	69

Source: Sedgwick (1974), p. 81.

control, particularly in the design and quality of the cars which were both important features of Fiat's marketing image. However, apart from a few essential bearings imported from Italy, all components were made by the U.S. plant which was largely self-sufficient.

The venture continued satisfactorily until 1914 and during that time the plant supplied all the demand for Fiats from the U.S.A. and some of the demand from Canada. By 1914, however, the plant had become completely dwarfed by the American manufacturers and the demand for cars had swung away from the Fiat image to the mass-produced one. Although the factory was still profitable the future did not look too promising — by 1915 Fiat were not even among the largest 15 car manufacturers in the U.S.A. In 1918, an opportunity arose and was taken, to sell the factory to the Duesenberg Motors Corporation for the production of aero engines. Fiat were supposed to retain a section of the plant to continue car production but this never happened, and in 1920 when Fiats reappeared for sale in the U.S.A. part of the advertising message was that they were completely made in Turin. After the sale of the plant, Fiat continued to sell, very profitably, about 500 cars each year in the U.S.A. at between $4500 and $6500 each.

Fiat also licensed production in Austria and a company called Austro-Fiat commenced production in Vienna in 1907. Here, Fiat had no stake in the company other than their entitlement to royalties. This situation continued, in spite of World War I, until 1921 when connections were finally severed.

An even less tangible connection existed with Fiat Motors Ltd in the U.K. This was established in 1903 by two Englishmen, D'Arcy Baker and Victor Miller, with a capital of £15,000 which increased in 1905 to £60,000. Although the factory was established with Fiat's approval, it was not and never became Turin-owned, but it successfully sold, serviced and repaired imported Fiats and produced English Fiats from chassis and engines imported from Italy, many of which were then re-exported to such diverse markets as Portugal, South America and Japan.

The Fiat company's involvement in the U.S.A. was, at least for the first few years, a success story. During that time they succeeded in making and selling cars in the U.S.A. against competition from France, Germany and the U.K., who were all exporting cars to the U.S. market, and against competition from America itself. Fiat succeeded because American production, when it first started in the U.S.A., was on a relatively small scale and because their luxury, high-powered and high-priced cars were suitable for the U.S. market. Fiat moved to the U.S.A. when their sales there justified domestic production and enabled the company to avoid the cost of shipping cars from Italy. The move also enabled the Italian plant to concentrate on satisfying European demand.

The failure of their U.S. plant was due to the advent of mass production and the creation of the cheap and simple car. The Americans, who had a considerable lead over European manufacturers in the automation of the car production process, were the first to introduce this new concept in cars. The availability of cars to a new mass market meant a lessening of demand for the craftsmen-built type of car that Fiat were making. In the end, Fiat bowed to the inevitable and although still profitable, their plant was sold when the opportunity arose and they reverted to exporting to the U.S.A. It was several years before Fiat themselves began to make a cheap mass-produced car.

Fiat's American venture was the only one in which they had a stake and even then it was very much a minority one. The only other overseas operation before 1914 was in Austria but that was strictly a licensed production scheme. Fiat did not embark on overseas investments again until the 1930s.

5.7   SOLVAY ET CIE (BELGIUM)[11]

The history of Solvay et Cie in America began with the imposition of tariffs by the Americans on alkali imported into their country. The first of these was the McKinley tariff of 1892 which was followed 5 years later by the Dingley tariff. Between the two of them, they effectively stopped the importing of alkali into the U.S.A. Before this, much of the imported alkali came from the U.K. firm of Brunner, Mond who were then the largest manufacturers of alkali in the world and half of whose sales were in the U.S.A.

Brunner, Mond had been established in 1873 to work the recently developed Solvay ammonia-soda process in the U.K. The patents for this process, which represented a tremendous improvement in the efficiency of alkali production, were held by the Belgian company Solvay et Cie. Solvay were a private company established in 1873 and they had taken a large but minority shareholding in Brunner, Mond at its foundation. The British company was, however, not ready for this sudden and disastrous loss of business and they immediately attempted to recoup this lost business by developing their embryonic Far-Eastern trade. They were in fact quite successful in this but it left the way open for Solvay, who had suffered a similar experience in Germany 20 years before, to develop their investment in the U.S.A. This was the Solvay Process Company and had been established in the U.S.A. in 1881 as a direct result of the German experience. It was a joint venture with American partners. Brunner, Mond themselves held 2000 $100 shares, although these had been arranged to give income rather than any degree of control. The Americans were headed by William Cogswell in alliance with Rowland Hazard and his family. They had succeeded in the U.S.A. in much the same way as Brunner, Mond had in the U.K. The American partners reached a satisfactory agreement with Solvay for the exploitation of the new process. Part of the appeal to Solvay was that the agreement would prevent the possibility of loss of trade in the U.S.A. in the event of the imposition of tariffs by the Americans, which was what had happened in Germany. The Solvay Process Company had a factory built at Syracuse, New York where brine, limestone, waterways and railroads, all essential to the efficient production of soda, were available nearby.

Although the tariffs that so disastrously affected Brunner, Mond were not operational until 1892, the company, because of its investment in the Solvay Process Company, had been gradually handing over sections of their U.S. export business to the latter since 1887. The tariffs immediately led to a dramatic speeding up of this process which was finally completed in 1905. America then became part of a cartel system in chemicals similar to the one which had been in operation in Europe for some time. By surrendering their U.S. business to the Solvay Process Company, rather than another U.S. alkali producer, Brunner, Mond hoped to at least benefit from the increased profits of that company by their shareholding. In fact, the progress of the Solvay Process Company was dramatic: in 1886, only 5 years after its foundation, it had captured 14 per cent of the U.S. market and a year later its share had risen to 24.5 per cent. In 1900, the factory produced 270,000 tons, or 70 per cent of the total U.S. production of alkali, and by 1905 the Syracuse factory had become the largest soda plant in the world and a second factory had been built at Detroit.

This satisfactory situation continued until World War I, but in 1920, the company together with the General Chemical Company, Barrett & Company and National Aniline & Chemical Company, were taken over by the Allied Chemical & Dye Corporation. As a result, Solvay et Cie and Brunner, Mond held about 20 per cent of the new corporation. Brunner, Mond retained their share until 1926 when they became one of the founder companies of ICI and the holding passed to the new company. A few years later ICI disposed of it to Solvay et Cie which today still retain their stake in the American company.

The Solvay involvements in the U.S.A., and indeed elsewhere, were invariably commercial success stories. To a large extent Solvay could not go far wrong because they held the patents for a chemical process that made the previous one totally uneconomic, although its predecessor, the Leblanc process, continued after Solvay appeared because it produced valuable by-products which Solvay did not. As a result, although they themselves were not keen, at least in the short term, to invest abroad, they were subjected to many proposals for joint ventures by overseas businessmen who could see the potential for the new process in their own countries.

By 1914 Solvay were co-operating on a joint-venture basis in seven European countries including Russia, and in the U.S.A. (see Table 3.6). Although the U.S. subsidiary eventually became part of the Allied Chemical and Dye Corporation, Solvay have continued to maintain their interest, in the form of a 20 per cent stake in the holding company. The company did, however, surrender their stake in Brunner, Mond, their English plant, when it was taken over by ICI in 1926.

There is no doubt that Solvay were and still are one of the most successful of the early direct investors in the U.S.A. but it is only fair to add that the unique advantage that they possess in the form of their process was very largely the reason for this success. Solvay would not be in the position they are today had their process been only marginally more efficient than the Leblanc one and had they not been encouraged into investing abroad by foreign entrepreneurs. It is also clear that although Solvay's U.S. subsidiary was a great success, their other European investments, including Brunner, Mond in the U.K. were no less successful.

5.8 THE ANGLO-SWISS CONDENSED MILK COMPANY AND HENRI NESTLÉ (SWITZERLAND)[1,2]

The Anglo-Swiss Condensed Milk Company was founded in 1866 with a share capital of Sf100,000 at Cham, Switzerland by the American brothers Charles and George Page. The title 'Anglo-Swiss' was designed to appeal to

British nationalism, because the U.K. was intended to be the major market for Swiss produced condensed milk. The business was an immediate success and the company soon began to export in addition to supplying the home market.

To increase production, the company began to expand quite rapidly and two years after the Franco-Prussian War of 1870 ended, bought two more factories. Both were in Switzerland, one at Guin and the other at Gossau. In addition, a third factory was built at Chippenham, England in the same year because the U.K. market was then taking about 75 per cent of the total Anglo-Swiss production. Later, in 1872, the Gossau factory was closed to transfer the machinery to a factory that had been bought at Lindau in Bavaria and the first German production started soon afterwards.

In 1874, two more factories were acquired in England when the company took over the English Condensed Milk Company of London with factories at Aylesbury and Middlewich. A few years later, in 1880, to increase production in its existing plants, Anglo-Swiss increased its share capital from Sf4 million to Sf10 million. However, in spite of all these developments, the demand from the U.S.A. which had become one of the company's best export markets, reaching 16,000 cases of condensed milk each month by 1881, could still not be met by the European factories.

George Page, one of the company's co-founders, then decided that the time had come to establish a production in the U.S.A. In 1882, Anglo-Swiss bought a factory at Middletown, New York from the Orange County Milk Association. At that time, the Borden Company were the only U.S. producers of condensed milk of any note, but because of substantial imports, they did not control the market and Page was already thinking in terms of overtaking Borden in the U.S.A. He also produced condensed milk behind the U.S. tariff wall, an additional factor leading to the new subsidiary's viability.

Initially the venture was a great success and within a year production had to be increased by 50 per cent, but Page himself became preoccupied with the American operation and began to spend over half his time in the U.S.A. This neglect of the European scene led to the parent company falling behind their long-time rivals, Henri Nestlé, who from the beginning (1867) had concentrated on the baby-food market. (Anglo-Swiss began milk products manufacturing only in 1877.) At the same time, the Borden Company began to attack the new intruder, using their strong 'Eagle' brand name as well as its new low-price lines, and other U.S. companies began to appear on the scene. Almost at once the profits of the new subsidiary were reduced and before very long the European operation, itself in a certain amount of trouble, was subsidising the American one.

The creation of the American subsidiary came midway between the two abortive attempts at a merger between Anglo-Swiss and Nestlé, which had reverted from its founder to a new company in 1875. In 1881 Anglo-Swiss offered Sf1.5 million for control of Nestlé but this was rejected, and two years later in 1883, Page turned down an approach from Nestlé, in the mistaken belief that the latter was the weaker company.

In 1884 Page embarked on a policy of manufacturing in all the main markets because by this time Anglo-Swiss had largely outgrown Switzerland. In line with this policy and in spite of the poor start of the Middletown factory, a second factory was soon opened at Dixon, Illinois, but it was to be no more successful than the first. Around 1890 trading conditions in Europe were very bad and the subsidising of the American factories by the European ones became punitive. In addition, five other competitors came to the market with similar products in the same year that the Dixon plant was completed and sugar prices shot up. Borden had, in the meantime successfully adapted their brand sales to allow for the seasonal fluctuation of milk supply which was yet another problem facing Anglo-Swiss. Page, who was by now resident in the U.S.A., began to emulate Borden, but in 1891, with the American factories operating at only 25 per cent capacity, he was clearly losing the battle and a boardroom crisis developed. Page's direction based on production targets, with little thought to marketing, exacerbated the situation. Page and his brother managed to defeat a move to liquidate the U.S. factories and in 1892 conditions improved both in the U.S.A. and U.K., which led to 100 per cent increase in profits that year.

This trend continued, and in 1895 Anglo-Swiss bought the Scandinavian Condensed Milk Company with factories at Hamar and Sandesund, Norway. The following year an issue of 3.75 per cent debenture stock for Sf2.5 million was twice oversubscribed − but Europe was still having to subsidise U.S. losses. In 1897 two new factories were opened by Page, one at Staverton in the U.K. and one at Sterling, Illinois in the U.S.A., but 2 years later he died. Page's achievements were immense during the 33 years that he was in charge but there is no doubt that his personal direction of the three main divisions in Europe, the U.K. and the U.S.A. was, due to the impossibly high workload, often at their expense.

George Page was succeeded by his brother David who continued his policies. By 1900, two more plants had been opened in the U.S.A., but in the same year, after further boardroom disagreements, David resigned and George's son Fred took over. Fred had never agreed with his father and uncle but for years had fought to sell out to the Borden Company in the U.S.A. and merge with Nestlé at home. His arrival at the top meant this could now take place and in 1902 the whole of the Anglo-Swiss

U.S. operation was sold to Borden for $2 million and in 1905 a full merger with Nestlé was completed. The new company was called the Nestlé and Anglo-Swiss Condensed Milk Company and had an initial capital of Sf40 million.

Table 5.6 shows the location of the 18 factories that constituted the Anglo-Swiss and Nestlé combine at its formation in 1905. The Nestlé factory at Fulton, New York, which had been established in 1890, was its first overseas investment and as can be seen from the table the only one from a total of 18, that was in the U.S.A.

TABLE 5.6 Anglo-Swiss and Nestlé's overseas factories at the time of their merger in 1905

No. of factories per country	Anglo-Swiss	Nestlé
Switzerland	3	4
U.K.	4	1
Norway	2	1
U.S.A.	–	1
Germany	–	1
Spain	–	1
TOTAL	9	9

Source: Heer (1966), p. 89.

The Fulton plant was the direct result of American tariffs. For several years Nestlé had been successfully exporting their milk food to the U.S.A. but by 1890 increasing tariffs had forced them to build an ultra-modern plant in the U.S.A. which could operate behind the tariff wall and so avoid the duty.

The Nestlé factory in Norway was established at Kap in 1898 as a result of the purchase of the Norwegian Milk Condensing Company. The object of this purchase was principally the need for greater production, but Norway was also a relatively low-cost production area for milk products. This was followed in 1901 by the establishment of a Nestlé factory at Tutbury in the U.K. In common with the Anglo-Swiss Company, the U.K. represented the largest of any of Nestlé's markets, including Switzerland, and production locally had become essential by 1901. In 1903, a plant at Hasse, in Germany was built to combat tariffs and in 1905 another near Santander, Spain for the same reason. In addition, since 1888 Nestlé had embarked on a policy of setting up foreign sales subsid-

Eight Case Histories

iaries to replace local agents and by the time of the merger many of these non-manufacturing investments were in operation around the world.

In 1906, a year after the merger took place, the new company bought the Cressbrook Dairy Company of Brisbane, Australia. Again, it was the tariffs on imports that motivated this investment and it is interesting to note that it was particularly pointed out to shareholders that the purpose of the purchase was to safeguard a position already won and *not* to capture a new market, as had been the Anglo-Swiss intention in the U.S.A. a few years before. In 1910, Nestlé and Anglo-Swiss bought a controlling interest in the U.K. company Fussell & Co. Ltd and in 1912 they bought an interest in the Galak Condensed Milk Company of Rotterdam. In the same year a new factory for the production of the latest skimmed milk product was built. The only other foreign investment before 1914 was the building of additional production facilities at Ashbourne in the U.K. in 1913. Nestlé and Anglo-Swiss saw several advantages in the U.K. as an investment area. These were the relatively low cost of production, the possibility of the introduction of tariffs by the U.K. government, the excellent facilities for exporting and the access to new export markets such as the U.K. dominions.

Without exception all Nestlé and Anglo-Swiss overseas subsidiaries, both before and after the merger, were set up for one or both of two reasons. These were the threat to existing business that arose from the introduction of new tariffs and the need for additional production. The failure of the Anglo-Swiss U.S. venture was due to the fact that many American firms were being set up at that time and as a result, although demand was high, so was the level of competition. In addition, Anglo-Swiss never gained the upper hand over the Borden Company and tended to remain one step behind. Because of the cost of the continuing battle with Borden, the low profit margins forced on Anglo-Swiss by fierce competition, and prolonged operating at less than full capacity, the American operation was never a success. It was only the dogged determination of George Page to succeed in the U.S.A. and the profits from the other Anglo-Swiss subsidiaries that prevented the American operation from being closed long before it eventually was. The Nestlé subsidiary in the U.S.A. was producing milk food for infants and not condensed milk and was therefore not subject to such fierce competition. It was also established to satisfy existing demand, and for these reasons was a success. In spite of this, and as a result of a complicated agreement between Nestlé and the Swiss chocolate firm of Kohler and Peter arrived at before the 1905 merger, the American subsidiary was, in 1917, taken over by Lamont, Corliss and Company, the U.S.

and Canadian marketing agents for Kohler and Peter at that time. Nestlé reacquired an interest in the Fulton works in 1929 and regained complete control again in 1951.

It can be seen, therefore, that the Anglo-Swiss investments were never a success while the Nestlé investment, although eventually being sold, was always profitable under Nestlé's ownership.

5.9 SIEMENS & HALSKE AND A.E.G. (GERMANY)[13]

The Allgemeine Elektricitäts-Gesellschaft, or A.E.G. as it is better known, was established in 1887 from the assets and liabilities of the Deutsche Edison Company. This company had gone into voluntary liquidation as a means of simplifying what had become a complex system of companies with varying degrees of association. A.E.G. had an initial capital of DM12 million, of which DM1 million were subscribed by Siemens & Halske as the name of the company then was. The two companies had various trade agreements with each other and both expanded rapidly.

In March 1892, the Siemens & Halske Electric Company of America was founded,[14] in which Siemens and Halske had an appropriate interest. This move was intended to exploit certain of the German company's patents in the U.S.A. The initial capital was $500,000 and a factory was built in Chicago. Just over a year later, in June 1893, the capital was doubled and shared equally by Siemens & Halske and the Americans. In 1894, a new trading agreement between A. E. G. and Siemens & Halske was signed and, as it had been designed to do, it led to the complete separation of the two companies in 1898 although 1894 marked the end of A.E.G.'s production commitments to Siemens & Halske. A.E.G. then began to expand rapidly and Siemens & Halske, in order to get access to capital more easily and thus to keep up with A.E.G., became a limited company or Aktiengesellschaft in 1897.

Meanwhile, in the U.S.A. Henry Villard had, in 1889, merged four companies into the Edison General Electric Company. He achieved this only with the assistance of an American—German finance syndicate in which both the A.E.G. and the German bank had a stake. In 1892 Villard's new company merged with the Thomson-Houston Company and, because this was against Villard's wishes, A.E.G. withdrew their money and as a result, terminated their short-lived investment in the U.S.A.

The Siemens & Halske Electric Company of America could certainly have had a share of the increasing U.S. business if they had concentrated on their German patents and designs and had used their experience gained at home. However, after the first troublesome year and at the point when the capital was being doubled, Dr Berliner, who had been the guiding light in the foundation of the U.S. plant, was recalled to Germany. It is not clear whether Berliner had requested to be allowed to return or whether it was against his wishes, but it was to prove a costly move. In July 1894, the Chicago works were destroyed by fire and the firm had to make do with a temporary home in the Grant Locomotive works. A second source states that the fire took place in 1893.[15] After about 6 months of this arrangement the American joint founder called Meysenburg, who had replaced Berliner, tried to persuade the German parent firm to buy up Grant Locomotives and take over their production. The Berlin partners, however, turned down the suggestion because all available capital was being used for expansion in Germany and they did not have the resources to increase the U.S. capital to the $2 million that Meysenburg requested. The Americans then produced the requisite capital and went it alone, and the Berlin company lost effective control. In 1897 the capital was again increased and the company merged with the Pennsylvanian Iron Works, thereby being completely and irrevocably alienated from its original purpose. Siemens & Halske then began to withdraw their U.S. holding and in 1903 cancelled all outstanding agreements with the U.S. company. In 1904 they succeeded in legally forcing the American company to change their name, which had become by then meaningless and, in terms of what the company was actually doing, misleading.

Siemens & Halske were also involved in the firm of Siemens Brothers in England. This was founded as Siemens, Halske & Company, London, in 1858 as a three-way partnership between Siemens & Halske of Berlin, William Siemens and Newall & Company of England. Newall's share of the company was comparatively small but William Siemens, who was one of the original 11 Siemens brothers and had lived in England from 1844, and was to remain there until his death in 1883, was, under the partnership agreement, entitled to one-third of any profits. Most of the remaining profits were destined for Berlin. The company made submarine cables and overland telegraph lines and equipment and the first factory was at Millbank Row in Westminster.[16]

In 1860 Newall & Company dropped out after a disagreement and in 1863 the company moved to Woolwich. In 1864, after further disagreements and some dramatic losses, most of which were subsequently absorbed by Werner Siemens using his private capital, J. G. Halske retired from the London business. Three years later in 1867 he also retired from the management of the Berlin firm. In 1865 the name of the London firm was changed to Siemens Brothers and continued under the direction of the joint proprietors Werner and William Siemens.

A period of several good years followed with occasional dramatic losses in between, and not infrequent policy disagreements with Berlin. In 1880 the firm became a limited company and by 1883 the capital was £500,000. In 1899, the capital was increased to £600,000 and the company reorganised. Although the fortune of the company was founded on telegraphic equipment, one of their greatest achievements being the completion, in 1871, of the Indo-European Telegraphic Line, their main innovation was the dynamo. This offered a replacement for batteries and magnetos, and was first produced in England by Siemens Brothers in 1879, although a few had been imported from Germany before that date and had started to play a large part in the business. This development eventually led to the creation of the Siemens Brothers Dynamo Works Limited in Stafford in 1903 and London in 1906.[17]

The performance of both companies continued to be basically very satisfactory and Werner Siemens, who died in 1892, his family and successors continued to hold their stake in the companies until World War I. However, this stake was seized by the Public Trustee, after the commencement of the war, and in 1917 part of it was sold to C. B. Crisp & Company while the Stafford Works and the heavy electrical engineering side of the business of Siemens Brothers Dynamo Works Limited was sold to the English Electric Company in 1919.

The Berlin firm also had stakes in subsidiaries in Russia and France, the former being established in 1855[18] to counteract Russian tariffs levied on imported cable and telegraphic apparatus. The Germans are understood to have received assurances from court circles of government contracts before embarking on this investment. The French subsidiary Siemens Frères, founded in 1878, opened a factory at Passy in 1879 for the manufacture of electric lighting equipment. French patent laws compelled the production to be in France and the Germans felt that the anti-German feeling, following the Franco-German War of 1870–1, had died down sufficiently for the investment to be viable. To be as certain of acceptance as they could, Siemens & Halske arranged that the subsidiary was established by Siemens Brothers in London. In any event the investment was a disaster and after several years of court actions against the Compagnie Continentale Edison over patent rights, an attempt was made to sell Siemens Frères to the Edison Company. This effort failed and the company was liquidated in 1886 with considerable loss to both Siemens and Halske and Siemens Brothers.

The German firm enjoyed some moderate success in France after 1889 when they embarked on a joint venture with a French company to make public power stations equipped with Siemens & Halske-made machinery. They also had some success in Italy with licensing operations for the manufacture of calcium cyanamide with their own German-made machinery.

There is comparatively little similarity between the Siemens & Halske failures in the U.S.A. and France, the latter being an ill-fated and ill-conceived investment from the start. The American investment failed for two main reasons. First was the withdrawal of Berliner at a crucial time and the handing over of control to an American who did not have Siemens & Halske's interests at heart. Berliner went on to prove his ability by rising to the top of the German operation and should have been left in charge of the U.S. operation which he had started. Second, was the loss of direction of the U.S. company. If Siemens & Halske had concentrated on their German patents, designs and experiences, they could have achieved a satisfactory share of the expanding U.S. market. This loss of direction became irrevocable after the fire of 1894 but could perhaps have been halted earlier had the Germans maintained their original level of control. The U.K. plant was only a failure inasmuch as family arguments and insufficient control by the parent company eventually led to their withdrawal, although not to the severing of all connections which took place later at the outbreak of war. The firm itself was, and still is, although now under a different name, very successful.

With the exception of the U.K. investment, the Siemens & Halske foreign investments can be seen to have been very unsuccessful and the U.S. investment in particular, probably their worst. The U.K. investment, although successful in its own right, cannot be regarded as successful in terms of a wholly or partly owned German foreign investment of acceptable duration.

5.10 SUMMARY AND CONCLUSION

The summary and comparison of case histories can be shown in Table 5.7. From the case histories it is possible to draw several conclusions.

(1) There were three main motives that led the companies to invest in the U.S.A.

TABLE 5.7 Summary of case histories

Summary of issues	1. Lever Brothers	2. Courtaulds	3. Royal Dutch Shell	4. Nobel	5. Fiat
Was the investment a success prior to 1914?	Commercially no, but valuable experience gained	Yes	Yes	No, due to problems of control at a distance	Yes, for a short time
Did the investment survive World War I?	Yes	Yes	Yes	No, sold before 1914	No, sold in 1918
Does the investment survive today?	Yes	No, compulsorily sold during World War II	Yes	No	No
What was the main motive for the investment?	Local sales justified local production	Exploitation of patents and tariff avoidance	Action by competitors	Exploitation of patents	Local sales justified local production
Was the investment a joint venture?	No	No	No	Yes	Yes
Was the U.S. subsidiary the company's only foreign investment?	No, one of many	Yes, at that time	No, one of many	No, one of many	Yes, at that time
Were other overseas investments more successful?	Yes, prior to 1914 – they all were	–	No, the U.S. investment was as successful as any	Yes, U.S. investment was least successful	–

TABLE 5.7 Summary of case histories (*continued*)

Summary of issues	6. Solvay	7. Nestlé	7a. Anglo-Swiss	8. Siemens	8a. A.E.G.
Was the investment a success prior to 1914?	Yes	Yes	No, due to competition	No, due to problem control at a distance	No, too short-lived
Did the investment survive World War I?	Yes	Yes, but sold shortly after	No, sold before 1914	No, sold before 1914	No, sold before 1914
Does the investment survive today?	Yes, in a modified form	Yes, in a modified form	No	No	No
What was the main motive for the investment?	Exploitation of patents	Tariff avoidance	Local sales justified local production	Exploitation of patents	Exploitation of patents
Was the investment a joint venture?	Yes	No	No	Yes	Yes
Was the U.S. subsidiary the company's only foreign investment?	No, one of many	No, one of many	No, one of many	No, one of many	Not known
Were other overseas investments more successful?	No, the U.S. investment was as successful as any	No, the U.S. investment was as successful as any	Yes, prior to 1914 they all were	No, none were very successful	—

117

(a) The imposition of new tariffs or an increase in the levels of existing ones. This was the most common motive and even in cases where other motives were stronger it was very often present.
(b) The exploitation of technical advances. The 1870–1914 period was one where rapid development and commercialisation of major inventions was taking place such as electricity and its supply to the public and the internal combustion engine. The potential for the exploitation of these patents, often held for all the major developed countries, was enormous.
(c) The situation where export sales to a particular market had reached a level that justified production locally.

(2) The types of investment appear to have been fairly evenly spread between joint ventures and complete control. In joint ventures, however, the local stake was nearly always the majority one.

(3) The investments were not always successful and where they were not the reason was frequently a lack of control from Europe which allowed the Americans to gain the initiative. The Anglo-Swiss and Lever Brothers' investments were exceptions, the former failing due to under-estimation of the competition and the latter due to a lack of understanding of local tastes. This lack of understanding by Lever Brothers meant that its U.S. investment was not a financial success prior to 1914 but in terms of the marketing experience they gained and later put to use in Europe, it definitely was. It should also be mentioned that in the case where their investments failed the parent companies did not necessarily lose the capital involved. In all the failure cases discussed, the subsidiaries were sold rather than put into liquidation and the parent companies were able to recoup some, if not all, of their capital.

(4) In only two of the eight cases was the American investment the company's only overseas venture and in the majority of the others, it was only one of several. In the latter cases there were no examples where the American venture was significantly more successful than the others and in fact there were several instances, such as Anglo-Swiss, where it was significantly less so.

6 Conclusion

6.1 GENERAL

This book has been conerned with the interpretation of the meaning of direct investment and it has been established that direct investment, as it is defined today, was very much in its infancy before 1870, particularly with regard to European activity in America. Direct investment had begun to occur more often between 1870 and World War I, but it remained secondary to portfolio investment in terms of value, although direct investment, defined by the locus of decision-making, was of considerable importance. It has also been established that direct investment occurred where the market was imperfect and this was the situation that existed in the U.S.A. during the 1870–1914 period caused by, among other things, the frequent and very often high tariffs that successive American governments imposed on imported goods. In the majority of cases the tariffs were applied to protect and develop local infant industry. The possible motives that might have led European companies to invest in the U.S.A. were numerous but in the case histories discussed in Chapter 5 only three – the desire to avoid U.S. tariffs, the opportunity to exploit 'patents' and the need for local production to satisfy local demand – occurred regularly and the most frequent was the company's desire to avoid tariffs.

Among the case histories the only exception to these motives was Royal Dutch Shell. In Shell's case, their move into the U.S. market was the oligopolist's classic answer to a rival's movement into their own territory. Shell's competitor was Standard Oil and the market was the Far East.

During this period the U.K. dominated all types of investment in the U.S.A. In direct investment, the major countries involved were European with the U.K. the dominant country, but others, including Germany, France, Holland, Belgium and Switzerland, all made significant direct investments. As a percentage of total investments, direct investment was only 10 per cent at its maximum and when direct investment in manufacturing industry is considered on its own, the figure is smaller still. However, of the 1914 cumulative total of all world foreign investment to date,

90 per cent had occurred after 1870 and this fact emphasises the importance of the 1870–1914 period.

The actual number of companies involved in direct investment in manufacturing industry was very small in relation to those involved in all types of investment. In 1914, at the end of the period under discussion, the number was over 100. However, many European-controlled enterprises existed in the U.S.A. after 1870 that did not survive until 1914, so the total number that had been involved before 1914, or were still involved at 1914, was considerably higher and probably well over 100.

It is possible to identify a few specific industries as being more attractive to foreign investors than others but some investment did take place in nearly all U.S. industries. In very few industries, however, did foreign control reach a level high enough to cause concern to the Americans. One of these was the rayon industry where Courtaulds had virtually 100 per cent control of the American Viscose Corporation which then was the only U.S. domestic producer. That situation did not change to the Americans' satisfaction until World War II, when Courtaulds was forced by the U.K. government to sell their interests to the Americans.

The dyestuffs industry was also attractive, although here the American situation was similar to that of most other developed countries insofar as 90 per cent of the U.S. market was controlled by German producers, though through exports rather than a high level of inward investment. This situation changed in 1917 when the German productive assets in the U.S.A. were seized, exports to the U.S.A. stopped and an American domestic industry established to make good the subsequent shortage.

In many industries the British were dominant among foreign investors, but again there were some exceptions – for example the German presence in the American electrical industry. Other European countries' interests were on a smaller scale than those of Britain and Germany, and tended to be confined to one industry. The Belgian interest, for example, was principally in the chemical industry and the French and Dutch interests were the oil industry. The Swiss interest was mainly in the food industry although they did have a small stake in the dyestuffs industry.

One prominent factor is that the situation frequently occurred where one foreign-controlled enterprise dominated the other foreign-controlled affiliates in a particular industry. A good example of this is the position of Solvay in the U.S. chemical industry. Here there were several direct investments by British and German companies but they were all dwarfed by the Belgian company's subsidiary, the Solvay Process Company, which not only rapidly overtook the others in size but also survived the war and exists today although in a modified form. The case histories in Chapter 5 illustrate several similar examples.

European investments in the U.S.A. were either joint ventures or almost completely controlled by the inventor. It was common in joint ventures for local partners to have the majority of the shares and consequently the majority of the control. It is not possible to put a figure to the failure rate of the foreign investments, since many of them were taken over by the Americans within a few years of their creation and many were failures. A good example of this type of failure was that by Siemens and Halske in the U.S.A. Very few investments actually went bankrupt, most of the failures being sold, and Lever Brothers, although it was a financial failure at least until 1914, did contribute considerably to the company's marketing expertise and did eventually succeed.

The most common cause of failure of the manufacturing affiliates was lack of control by the parent companies due to distance and poor communication. The American investment seldom seems to have been the company's only overseas venture and among the case histories, only Courtaulds falls into that category. However, when the American investment was one of many overseas, it does not appear to have been significantly better than the others and in fact, in Lever Brothers, Anglo-Swiss and Nobel, it was significantly worse.

Finally, it is surprising, considering the size of the U.S. market at the start of the 1870–1914 period, its growth during those years and the generally favourable conditions for foreign investment that existed, how little foreign direct investment in U.S. manufacturing industry actually took place. The problems of communication and control at such a great distance, and their costs, must have been the principal reason for that situation. In many cases, company organisational structures were also unable to cope with the problems of investment at a great distance. Unincorporated branches began to give way to local incorporations and local decision-making began to replace the cumbersome system of referring decisions to head office. Similarly, financial structures were highly dependent on the source country and the marked absence of vigorous re-investment policies and the obstacles to raising capital in the host country contributed to failure.

6.2 THE IMPACT OF EUROPEAN DIRECT INVESTMENT ON THE DEVELOPMENT OF THE U.S.A.

Speaking of the period 1870–1914 Dunning said: 'These were the years of vast speculating investments in cattle raising, mining, land and breweries, projects which have long since been forgotten but which exerted a vital

TABLE 6.1 An estimate of the relative importance of foreign direct investment (F.D.I.) in the U.S.A., 1914 and 1919

	Capital stock	$ million 1914	1919
1.	Total capital in manufacturing (book value)	20,784	40,289
2.	Estimated total book value of foreign direct investment	1,292	899
3.	Estimated total book value of *European* direct investment	1,100	730
4.	F.D.I. as percentage of total (2 as percentage of 1)	6.2	2.2
5.	European direct investment as percentage of total (3 as percentage of 1)	5.6	1.8

Source: Lewis (1938), p. 546; United States Department of Commerce, Bureau of the Census (1960), *Historical Statistics of the United States,* Washington, D.C., various pages.

influence on U.S. economic development at that time'.[1] Perhaps now we are able to go a little further in our judgement of the impact of pre-World War I European direct investment on the development of the U.S.A.

Because of the paucity of accurate data, it is virtually impossible to give a quantitative estimate of the importance of European direct investment in those years. Lewis's estimated figures (see Table 6.4) give total foreign direct investment as 6.2 per cent of the book value of *manufacturing* industry in 1914, and 2.2 per cent of the same magnitude in 1919. European direct investment is 5.6 per cent and 1.8 per cent of the book value of manufacturing investment in these two years. However, Lewis's figures are not purely for manufacturing and are not complete, so this is a minimum estimate (see Table 6.1).

These bald figures do not illustrate the contribution of European direct investment to U.S. development. The inflow of technology inherent in the investment was in many sectors critically important. Markham notes that: 'Every profitable rayon venture in the United States began with some type of association with European firms'.[2] Outstanding among the successes of European F.D.I. was Courtaulds' U.S. subsidiary, the American Viscose Corporation. *Fortune* magazine commented in 1937: 'American Viscose, modest, secretive and unknown, is one of the industrial miracles of our times, a phenomenon comparable to Standard Oil, or the automobile empire of Henry Ford.'[3] This gives a good contemporary idea of the value of American Viscose before its forced divestment in World War II.

Conclusion

Similar importance must be attributed to European direct investment in the chemicals and dyestuffs industries, which before World War I were dominated by German interests. The expropriation of German industry in the U.S.A. by the Alien Property Custodian allowed the Americans to gain a foothold in their domestic industry from which time the Europeans have never been allowed to regain their former dominance.

The early creation of international competition in the oil industry, characterised by cross-penetration of markets by direct investment, is well illustrated by the cat-and-mouse tactics of Shell and Standard Oil. Shell Oil is, of course, still well established in the U.S.A. Other early European entrants who still have a dominant position in the U.S.A. include Unilever (the inheritor of the Lever Brothers' investments), Nestlé in the food industry and Coats and Clark Inc. in textiles. The European control of brewing, mining, land development and railways has long since evaporated, but there has recently (in the late 1970s) been a huge influx or re-influx of European direct investment in chemicals, automobiles, the electrical and electronic industries, food products, banking and the service industries.[4] Spence's comment on British capital serves well here: 'If the East—West flow of capital ebbed or was at least diverted after 1914, it was not until English pounds had made concrete contributions to the development of an American financial and industrial structure which largely eliminated the need for outside capital'.[5]

Then, as now, the value of patents and proprietory knowledge were vital components of success in foreign direct investment. Past innovations were critical as was the secrecy element — the German patents system up to World War II has been described as a system for stealing foreign secrets and keeping their own.[6] The transplanting of European innovations occurred by many means, including direct investment which was one of the most important and probably the one which gave greatest potential for the innovators, via internal use of the advantage, to reap the greatest reward.

6.3 AFTERMATH OF WORLD WAR I

In the summer of 1914, the U.S.A. was a debtor nation. At the end of the war she was a net creditor. Table 6.2 illustrates this and also shows that Foreign Direct Investment (F.D.I.) in the U.S.A. did not regain its pre-war level until 1929. Table 6.2 also shows that by 1914, the U.S.A.

TABLE 6.2 Net asset position of the U.S.A., 1869–1935 (All figures in current $ million)

Year	1869	1897 31 Dec.	1908 31 Dec.	1914 1 July	1919 31 Dec.	1924 31 Dec.	1929 31 Dec.	1935 31 Dec.
Assets								
Private *total*	75*	685	2,525	3,514	6,956	10,754	17,009	13,694
of which F.D.I.	75*	635	1,639	2,652	3,880	5,389	7,553	7,219
Liabilities								
Private *total*	1,540	3,395	6,400	7,200	3,985	4,044	8,931	6,329
of which F.D.I.	1,390*	3,145*	6,000*	1,310	900	975	1,400	1,580

* 'Securities and direct investments'

Source: Derived from tables in Lewis (1938), Chapter XXI.

Conclusion

had substantial F.D.I. assets and was indeed, on F.D.I. alone, a net creditor nation ($2,652 million outward against $1,310 million inward F.D.I.).

World War I was a watershed not only in the U.S. creditor/debtor position, but also in the amount and orientation of European direct investment. In 1915 the U.K. Treasury instructed the Bank of England to buy U.S. securities in London for sale in New York. The American Dollar Securities Committee published a 'wanted list' of assets to acquire and the greatest liquidation occurred in railway securities. Portfolio investment was easier to liquidate than direct investment so much British direct investment in the U.S.A. survived World War I. In July 1914 British-controlled enterprises in the U.S.A. accounted for 'perhaps 600 million dollars . . . or as much as all other foreign-controlled enterprises in the country combined. By the end of 1919 some few of the companies had been sold, but control of most of them was still with the British'.[7]

The change in British foreign-direct investment occurred because of a change in attitude and therefore in orientation. The focus had already changed over time — in the 1880s Australia, Argentina and the U.S.A. were the main recipients, after 1900 Canada and the U.S.A. In 1913 an estimated 20 per cent of British (total) foreign investment was in the U.S.A. In 1930 this proportion had dropped to 5 per cent with a far greater concentration on countries of the British Empire (see Table 6.3). Even by 1930 British foreign investments had not regained their 1913 levels. Stopford suggests that:

> The evidence indicates that most of the very early (U.K.) manufacturing investments were in Europe and the United States. Only during the 1920s and 1930s did an Empire, or later on a Commonwealth, preference in investment become a predominant influence on location decisions.[8]

The greater part of French direct investments were thrown on to the market during the war. Examples are the Southern Aluminum Company (a $5.5 million investment which was sold early in 1915), a large French interest in the Mid-West Refining Company was sold to Standard Oil of Indiana some time between 1917 and 1920, and a large French interest in Union des Petroles d'Oklahoma (valued at $8 million) was bought up by the Pure Oil Company between 1918 and 1922. Lewis comments: 'little remained (in the United States) except the properties needed for facilitating French trade with the United States'.[9]

Firms and individuals from the Netherlands sold many classes of U.S. securities, but Royal Dutch-Shell had increased its investment in California

TABLE 6.3 Distribution of British foreign investments, 1913 and 1930

Areas of the world	1913 (%)	1930 (%)
British Empire	47	59
U.S.A.	20	5
South America	20	21
Europe	6	8
Rest of world	7	7
TOTAL	100	100
TOTAL (£ million)	(4000)	(3000)

Source: Alice Teichova (1974), *An Economic Background to Munich,* Cambridge University Press, p. 5.

from $17.7 million in 1914 to $38.5 million by the end of 1919. Swiss investment in the U.S.A. actually increased after the U.S.A. entered the war.

There was considerable liquidation of German (and allied states') property. Of the $950 million total invested in the U.S.A. before the war, about $550 million of German investment remained at the close of 1919. These were claims of German nationals against an American Government officially acting as trustee for their confiscated property.

The position is summarised in Table 6.4, which gives a maximum valuation of European direct investment as $800 million in 1919 (including Alien Custodian holdings) compared with over $1.1 billion in 1914. There is a clear presumption that the period 1914–20 saw a change in the balance of world economic power away from Europe, and particularly the U.K., towards the U.S.A.[10] in which this liquidation and expropriation of European assets played an important part. Only today are European firms re-establishing themselves as major direct investors in the U.S.A.

World War I also cut the U.S.A. off from European exporters. This had important repercussions in a number of industries. In manufacturing, the American Smelting and Refining Company built a large plant at Perth Amboy to replace German imports. In glass, virtually a new industry was created — before the War Belgium had been the major supplier of imported plate and window glass and Germany of optical glass. Many new mineral-extracting and refining plants were started during the war and protected

TABLE 6.4 Book value of foreign countries' direct investments in the U.S.A., in 1914 and 1919

Creditor country	$ million 1 July 1914	31 Dec. 1919
U.K.	600	500
Germany	300	*
Netherlands	136	160
Canada	132	169
France	45	20
Austria-Hungary, Bulgaria, Turkey	30	*
All others	50	50
TOTAL	1,292	899
TOTAL EUROPE (approx.)	1,160	730

* Property still held by Alien Property Custodian valued at $65.8 million.

Source: Lewis (1938), p. 546.

by tariffs and subsidies after it. The U.S.A. steel, iron and munitions industries were stimulated by European orders for war supplies.

Perhaps the most important industrial consequences occurred in the chemicals and dyestuffs industries where, before the war, Germany had a virtual monopoly. After U.S. entry into the war (1917), many German-owned patents were confiscated and placed in American hands by the Alien Property Custodian. The patents were then sold to a fiduciary corporation, organised for the purpose, called the Chemical Foundation. Four to five thousand patents were granted to licensed private manufacturers (after the war the legality of this process was challenged in the courts without success). A virtually new domestic industry was created and by the end of the war domestic U.S. production was meeting the demand, although quality was still not equal to the German products because of the difficulty of implementing skilfully disguised German patents.[11] Dyestuffs and explosives were, of course, allied products in that many of the intermediate products were common. Consequently the strategic importance of the industry gave the rationale for tariff protection after the war. In relation to the interrelated investment of I.G. Farben, the company formed by the amalgamation of Bayer and BASF among others, and Metallgesellschaft, wrangling over return (or compensation) of seized assets continued until July 1938. Attempts to disguise ownership of

German assets through a Swiss intermediary led to numerous court cases in one of which Alien Property Custodian Miller was convicted of fraud.[12]

American dependence on foreign imports was vastly reduced by the infant industry strategies which were partly enforced by the war and shrewd post-war policy.

6.4 CONCLUSION

Teichova states that: 'changes in the economic structure in the inter-war period appear to have foreshadowed the post-war economic predominance of the powerful multinational companies'.[13] This comment, with reference to the formation of huge 'trusts' and interpenetration of European markets, would be much weaker were it transposed to the period before World War I, but it would still retain some truth and value. European direct investment in the U.S.A. contained the beginnings of the worldwide flows of investment observed in the world economy today. The problems of communications, control, also unsatisfactory corporate structures and management techniques were much greater in that period before telephone, telex and video systems, but essentially the problems of adaptation of product, marketing, organisational structures and general management existed then and executives in that era did not have the accumulated experience of management 'at a distance' which exists today. Given these problems, it is not surprising that many ventures resulted in failure, or at least absorption into ownership by domestic industry.

Current theories of the behaviour of multinational firms stand up well to the task of explaining pre-World War I investment in the U.S.A. The role of market imperfections, location theory elements and internalisation of markets all appear to be relevant in the analysis of the flow of F.D.I. to the U.S.A. High levels of protectionism, the desire to control raw materials or critical intermediate goods inputs, exploitation of internal proprietary knowledge created by past investments in R&D and least-cost location practices all applied in the industries and case histories which we have been able to analyse. Differences arise from the vastly greater 'costs of doing business abroad', which provided an insuperable barrier for many potential and 'failed' direct investments. Perhaps also the entrepreneurial spirit of the dominant figures (e.g. Samuel, Lever) should be emphasised in contrast to the 'corporate planning' approach of today's multinationals. It may be that some of the failures would have been avoided by application of a more cautious 'planning' procedure, but this may have eliminated some of the successes too — particularly those which provided a base for later expansion and consolidation in the U.S.A. The learning experiences of the early investments cannot be overestimated for its value in the development of techniques of foreign market servicing, which the European companies came to employ worldwide.

Notes and References

NOTES TO CHAPTER 1: DIRECT INVESTMENT

1. G. Ragazzi (1973), 'Theories of the Determinants of Direct Foreign Investments', *I.M.F. Staff Papers*, vol. XX, no. 2, July.
2. C. P. Kindleberger (1969), *American Business Abroad* (New Haven, Conn.: Yale University Press).
3. John M. Stopford (1974), 'The Origins of British-based Multinational Manufacturing Enterprises', *Business History Review*, vol. XLVIII, no. 3, pp. 303–35. It should be noted, however, that in many cases, 'practically all the capital invested [in the cotton industry] by foreign-born manufacturers [before 1830] was amassed in America'. Caroline F. Ware (1931), *The Early New England Cotton Manufacture* (New York: Russell & Russell). The quotation is from p. 129.
4. Peter Svedberg (1978), 'The Portfolio-Direct Composition of Private Foreign Investment in 1914 Revisited', *Economic Journal*, vol. LXXXVIII, no. 4, December.
5. T. C. Coram (1967), 'The Role of British Capital in the Development of the United States, 1600–1914' (unpublished M.Sc. thesis, University of Southampton). See especially Chapter 22.
6. Michael Z. Brooke and H. Lee Remmers (1970), *The Strategy of Multinational Enterprises* (London: Longman).
7. Kindleberger (1970), pp. 1–36.
8. M. Edelstein (1974), 'The Determinants of UK Industry Abroad, 1870–1913: The US Case', *Journal of Economic History*, vol. 34, no. 4, December.
9. Coram (1967), pp. 232 and 342.
10. Alice Teichova (1974), *An Economic Background to Munich: International Business and Czechoslovakia 1918–38* (Cambridge: Cambridge University Press).
11. Peter J. Buckley and Mark Casson (1976), *The Future of the Multinational Enterprise* (London: Macmillan).
12. Buckley and Casson (1976). See also Ian H. Giddy (1978), 'The Demise of the Product Cycle Model in International Business Theory', *Columbia Journal of World Business*, vol. XIII, no. 1, Spring, and the pioneering article by R. H. Coase (1937), 'the Nature of the Firm', *Economica*, vol. 4, pp. 386–405.
13. The dangers surrounding the inadequate introduction of technology via licensing are admirably illustrated by the delay in the successful introduction of the diesel engine into the U.S.A. via a patent monopoly. The lack of control from the source country contributed to this. See R. H. Lytle (1968), 'The Introduction of Diesel Power into the

United States, 1897–1912', *Business History Review*, vol. XLII, no. 2 (Summer).

NOTES TO CHAPTER 2: PRELIMINARY ANALYSIS

1. R. Nurske (1954), 'The Problems of International Investment Today in the Light of 19th Century Experience', *Economic Journal*, vol. LXIV, December, pp. 744–58.
2. John H. Dunning (1970), 'British Investment in the United States 1860/1913', Chapter 4 in *Studies in International Investment* (London: Allen & Unwin).
3. Dunning (1970), p. 22.
4. Brinley Thomas (1967), 'The Historical Record of International Capital Movements to 1913' in J. H. Adler (ed.), *Capital Movements and Economic Development* (London; Macmillan), pp. 3–32. Reprinted in John H. Dunning (ed.) (1972), *International Investment* (Harmondsworth: Penguin).
5. Peter Svedberg (1978). See also Chapter 1, Section 2.
6. Dunning (1970), p. 18.
7. Cleona Lewis (1938), *America's Stake in International Investments* (Washington: The Brookings Institution), p. 546.
8. E. Staley (1935), *War and the Private Investor* (Chicago: Chicago University Press).
9. Dunning (1970), p. 17.
10. Thomas (1967), pp. 34–6 in Dunning (1972).
11. Ibid., p. 34 in Dunning (1972).
12. Dunning (1970), p. 17.
13. Lewis (1938), p. 124.
14. Staley (1935), p. 11.
15. Dunning (1970), pp. 152–3.
16. Douglass C. North (1960), 'The United States Balance of Payments, 1790–1860', in *Trends in the American Economy in the 19th Century* (Princeton, New Jersey: Princeton University Press).
17. Dunning (1970), p. 153.

NOTES TO CHAPTER 3: HISTORICAL BACKGROUND

1. J. S. Davis (1917), *Essays in the Earlier History of American Corporations* (Cambridge, Mass: Harvard University Press), vol. II, pp. 264, 280.
2. Lewis (1938), p. 69.
3. John H. Dunning (1961), 'British Investment in U.S. Industry', *Moorgate and Wall Street,* Autumn, pp. 5–23.
4. Ibid., p. 9.
5. Constance McClaughlin Green (1951), 'Light Manufactures and the Beginnings of Precision Manufacture', in Harold F. Williamson (ed.),

The Growth of the American Economy, 2nd edition (Englewood Cliffs: Prentice-Hall).
6. David J. Jeremy (1973), 'British Textile Technology Transmission to the United States: The Philadelphia Region Experience 1770–1820', *Business History Review,* vol. XLVII, no. 1. See also 'Samuel Slater and the American Textile Industry 1789–1835', Section XVI in N. S. B. Gras and Henrietta M. Larson (eds.) (1939) *Casebook in American Business History* (New York: F. S. Crofts).
7. Dunning (1961), p. 8.
8. D. S. McClain (1974), 'Foreign Investment in U.S. Manufacturing and the Theory of Direct Investment' (unpublished doctoral thesis, Massachusetts Institute of Technology, September), pp. 46–50. Also Dunning (1961), p. 8.
9. R. W. Hidy (1949), *The House of Baring in American Trade and Finance* (Cambridge, Mass.: Harvard University Press).
10. McClain (1974), p. 84.
11. Lewis (1938), p. 68.
12. Douglass C. North (1963), 'Industrialisation in the United States', in W. W. Rostow (ed.), *The Economics of Take-Off into Sustained Growth* (London: Macmillan). For a good example of the development of stages of industry see Blanche E. Hazard (1921), *The Organisation of the Boot and Shoe Industry in Massachusetts before 1875* (Cambridge, Mass.: Harvard University Press).
13. Rolla Milton Tyron (1917), *Household Manufactures in the United States, 1640–1860* (Chicago: University of Chicago Press).
14. Glenn Porter and Harold C. Livesay (1971), *Merchants and Manufacturers* (Baltimore: Johns Hopkins Press), passim.
15. Dunning (1970), 'British Investment in the United States 1860/1913', in Dunning (1970).
16. McClain (1974), Chapter 1.
17. See A. H. John (1959), *A Liverpool Merchant House: Being the History of Alfred Booth and Company* (London: Allen & Unwin).
18. M. Edelstein (1974), 'The Determinants of UK Investment Abroad, 1870–1913: The US Case', *Journal of Economic History,* vol. 34, no. 4, December, pp. 980–1007.
19. For further discussion of the reconstruction of the post-bellum South see Kenneth M. Stampp (1966), *The Era of Reconstruction, 1869–77* (New York: Alfred A. Knopf).
20. North (1963). See also D. L. Burn (1931), 'The Genesis of American Engineering Competition, 1850–1870', *Economic History,* vol. II, January 1931. Burn points out that Britain was already importing machinery and technology from the U.S. in this period and notes the effect of education on U.S. industrial development.
21. H. Wayne Morgan (1971), *Unity and Culture: The United States, 1877–1900* (Harmondsworth: Pelican).
22. Dunning (1970), p. 149.
23. R. Vernon (1971), *Sovereignty at Bay* (London: Longman).
24. E. V. Morgan and W. A. Thomas (1962), *The Stock Exchange, its History and Functions* (London: Elek Books).

Notes and References 133

25. Victor S. Clark (1929), *History of Manufactures in the United States*, vol. II (New York: McGraw-Hill).
26. W. H. B. Court (ed.) (1965), *British Economic History 1870–1914: Commentary and Documents* (Cambridge: Cambridge University Press).
27. Coram (1967), p. 329.
28. Ibid., p. 331.
29. Dunning (1961), p. 9.
30. Ibid., p. 10.
31. Arthur H. Rosenbloom (1976), *Buying and Selling Businesses: The Past Shapes the Future* (New York: Standard Research Consultants), is the major source for the following two paragraphs. Also Joe S. Bain (1951), 'Industrial Concentration and Anti-Trust Policy', in H. F. Williamson (ed.), *The Growth of the American Economy* (Englewood Cliffs: Prentice-Hall) and A. D. H. Kaplan (1964), *Big Enterprise in a Competitive System* (Washington: The Brookings Institution).
32. *Northern Securities Co. v. United States*, 193 US 197 (1904).
33. *United States v. American Tobacco Co.*, 221 US 106 (1911); *Standard Oil Co. (New Jersey) v. United States*, 221 US 1 (1911).
34. Ralph Nelson (1959), *Merger Movements in American Industry, 1895–1956* (Princeton, New Jersey: Princeton University Press).
35. Peter J. Buckley and Mark Casson (1976).
36. Porter and Livesay (1971), p. 215.
37. Contrast Donald G. Paterson (1976), *British Direct Investment in Canada, 1870–1904: Estimates and Determinants* (Toronto: University of Toronto Press).
38. Vernon (1971), p. 83.
39. Ibid., p. 84.
40. Dunning (1961), p. 9.
41. L. G. Franko (1976), *The European Multinationals* (London: Harper & Row).
42. Barry E. Supple (ed.) (1963), 'Introduction to Part IV – The Transformation of a Continent', in *The Experience of Economic Growth* (New York: Random House).
43. All figures from United States Department of Commerce, Bureau of the Census (1960), *Historical Statistics of the United States*, Washington DC.
44. Bureau of the Census (1960), p. 139.
45. 'The Development of Internal Markets: Metropolitan Economic', Section XXV in N. S. B. Gras and Henrietta Larson (1939).
46. L. G. Franko (1974), 'The Origins of Multinational Manufacturing by Continental European Firms', *Business History Review*, vol. XLVIII, no. 3, pp. 277–302.
47. Stopford (1974), pp. 303–35.
48. Lewis (1938), p. 102.
49. Franko (1976), p. 9.
50. Information on Reckitt's from Basil N. Reckitt (1965), *The History of Reckitt and Sons Limited*. (London: A. Brown & Sons).
51. Information on Green's from Green's of Wakefield (1956), *Waste Not:*

The Story of Green's Economiser (London: Harley Publishing Co.), p. 110.
52. Ibid.
53. G. W. Crutchley (1921), *John Mackintosh: A Biography* (London: Hodder & Stoughton).
54. Harold V. Mackintosh (1966), *By Faith and Work* (autobiography) (London: Hutchinson).
55. Lewis (1938), pp. 570–2.
56. W. Rupert MacLaurin (1949), *Invention and Innovation in the Radio Industry* (New York: Macmillan Inc.).
57. Ibid., p. 50.
58. Ibid., p. 39.

NOTES TO CHAPTER 4: REVIEW BY INDUSTRY

1. L. F. Haber (1958), *The Chemical Industry During the 19th Century* (Oxford: Clarendon Press).
2. J. J. Beer (1959), *The Emergence of the German Dye Industry* (Urbana, Illinois: Illinois University Press).
3. Haber (1958), p. 130.
4. Raymond Vernon (1971).
5. Christopher Tugendhat (1971), *The Multinationals* (London: Eyre & Spottiswoode).
6. J. R. Geigy AG (Undated), *200 Years Geigy* (Basel: J. R. Geigy A.G.).
7. McClain (1974), pp. 43–4.
8. Beer (1959), p. 125.
9. W. J. Reader (1970), *I.C.I.: A History*, vol. I (London: Oxford University Press), See also Richard Sasuly (1947), *I. G. Farben*, (New York: Boni and Gaer); and Joseph Borkin (1979), *The Crime and Punishment of I. G. Farben* (London: André Deutsch).
10. McClain (1974), p. 39.
11. L. F. Haber (1971), *The Chemical Industry, 1900–1930* (Oxford: Clarendon Press), p. 27.
12. Haber (1958), p. 148–9.
13. Haber (1971), pp. 27–8.
14. Haber (1958), p. 151.
15. Haber (1971), p. 179. See also John G. Glover and William B. Cornell (eds.) (1951) *The Development of American Industries*, 3rd edition (New York: Prentice-Hall).
16. McClain (1974), p. 43.
17. Nicholas Faith (1971), *The Infiltrators* (London: Hamish Hamilton). See also Glover and Cornell (1951), p. 423.
18. Clark (1929).
19. McClain (1974), p. 37.
20. A. Plummer (1951), *International Combines in Modern Industry*, 3rd edition (London: Pitman).
21. Clark (1929), *op. cit.*, p. 932. See also T. C. Coram (1967), 'The

Role of British Capital in the Development of the United States 1600–1914' (unpublished masters thesis, Southampton University), p. 345.
22. The object of the amalgamation was 'to unite the business of the manufacture of spool, crochet, knitting, mending and other cottons, including the allied businesses of cotton spinning, doubling, twisting, dyeing, bleaching, polishing and spool making', i.e. to achieve fully integrated production internally and also to concentrate production in the most profitable plants, closing the smaller ones. Melvin Thomas Copeland (1917), *The Cotton Manufacturing Industry of the United States* (New York: Augustus Kelley), pp. 169–70.
23. Lewis (1938), pp. 100–1.
24. Copeland (1917), p. 340. Quotation from *The Economist*, 2 November 1907, p. 1865.
25. 'Coats & Clark USA', *The News Reel*, September 1966 (Coats & Clark house magazine).
26. Coram (1967), p. 350. See also J. W. Markham (1962), *Competition in the Rayon Industry* (Cambridge, Mass.: Harvard University Press), pp. 14–17.
27. Arthur Harrison Cole (1926), *The American Wool Manufacture* (Cambridge, Mass.: Harvard University Press). The quotations are from vol. 2, p. 163.
28. Lewis (1938), p. 529. See also Max W. Stoehr (1928), 'The Wool Industry' in H. T. Warshaw (ed.), *Representative Industries in the United States* (London: Allen & Unwin).
29. Lewis (1938), p. 94.
30. C. Tugendhat and A. Hamilton (1975), *Oil, The Biggest Business* (London: Eyre Methuen).
31. Lewis (1938), p. 95.
32. Ibid., pp. 95–6.
33. McClain (1974), p. 33.
34. Coram (1967), p. 331.
35. Lewis (1938), p. 99.
36. Ibid., p. 99.
37. G. Paish (1911), 'Great Britain's Capital Investments in Individual, Colonial and Foreign Countries', *Journal of the Royal Statistical Society*, vol. LVIV, no. 1, January.
38. Coram (1967), pp. 333–4.
39. A. Emil Davies (1928), *Foreign Investments* (London: A. W. Shaw). The quotation is from p. 65.
40. McClain (1974), p. 36. The enterprise failed after the death of its promoters.
41. Clark C. Spence (1958), *British Investments and the American Mining Frontier, 1860–1901* (New York: Cornell University Press).
42. McClain (1974), p. 37.
43. McClain (1974), p. 32. See also note 64.
44. Ibid., p. 31. See also F. E. Richter (1927), 'The Copper Mining Industry in the United States, 1845–1925', *Quarterly Journal of Economics*, vol. XLI, nos. 1 and 3, February and August.

45. Lewis (1938), p. 83.
46. Ibid., p. 85.
47. Ibid., p. 87.
48. Ibid., pp. 568–70.
49. Edward P. Crapol (1973), *America for Americans* (Westport, Connecticut: Greenwood Press). The quotation is taken from p. 92.
50. Crapol (1973), pp. 104–5.
51. W. M. Pearce (1964), *The Matador Land and Cattle Company* (Norman, Oklahoma: Oklahoma University Press). See also W. Turrentine Jackson (1968), *The Enterprising Scot* (Edinburgh: Edinburgh University Press).
52. Pearce (1964), p. viii.
53. Information on Bryant & May's venture kindly supplied in personal communication to authors from Mr G. MacFarlane, Company Secretary, dated 6 February 1979.
54. Copy of letter from Diamond Match Co. to Bryant & May dated 29 January 1904.
55. Charles Byron Kuhlmann (1929), *The Development of the Flour Milling Industry in the United States* (Boston: Houghton Mifflin), p. 134.
56. Kuhlmann (1929), p. 171.
57. Plummer (1951), p. 84.
58. G. Porter and H. C. Livesey (1971), pp. 201–8.
59. Maurice Corina (1975), *Trust in Tobacco* (London: Michael Joseph), p. 102.
60. Ibid., p. 102. See also Richard B. Tennant (1950), *The American Cigarette Industry* (New Haven, Conn.: Yale University Press).
61. Faith (1971), p. 64.
62. Corina (1975), p. 75.
63. Plummer (1975), p. 41.
64. Information kindly supplied by Metallgesellschaft, A.G., Frankfurt.
65. Lewis (1938), p. 101. See also Victor S. Clark (1929), vol. II.
66. Coram (1967), p. 346.
67. Ibid., p. 348.
68. Faith (1971), Chapter 6.
69. Plummer (1951), p. 5.
70. McClain (1974), p. 36.
71. Lewis (1938), p. 102.
72. L. T. Wells Jr. (1974), 'Automobiles', in R. Vernon (ed.), *Big Business and the State* (London: Macmillan).
73. L. G. Franko (1974).
74. Wells (1974), p. 231.
75. Leland H. Jenks (1971), *The Migration of British Capital to 1875* (London: Nelson).
76. Leland H. Jenks (1951), 'Britain and American Railway Development', *Journal of Economic History*, vol. XI, no. 4, Autumn.
77. Dorothy E. Adler (1970), *British Investment in American Railways, 1834–1898* (Charlottesville: University Press of Virginia). See conclusion for appraisal of the extent of British control over U.S. railways.

Notes and References 137

78. Lewis (1938), p. 87.
79. McClain (1974), p. 28.
80. Faith (1971). On the role of the 'Anglo-American' Bankers in financing U.S. development see Ralph W. Hidy (1941), 'The Organisation and Functions of Anglo-American Merchant Bankers, 1815–60', *Journal of Economic History*, 1941 Supplement.
81. On Scottish investment see Jackson (1968), and Bruce Lenman and Kathleen Donaldson (1971), 'Partners' Incomes, Investment and Diversification in the Scottish Linen Area, 1850–1921', *Business History*, vol. XIII, no. 1, January.
82. The history of Booth's is drawn from A. H. John (1959).
83. Information on the antecedents of BBA Group's investment is taken from a personal communication to the authors dated 12 February 1980 from Mr D. M. Pearson, Chairman, BBA Group Ltd.
84. Lewis (1938), pp. 142, 570.
85. Franko (1976), p. 166.
86. Peter Mathias (1967), *Retailing Revolution* (London: Longman).
87. Thomas J. Lipton (1931), *Leaves from the Lipton Logs* (London: Hutchinson). This is Lipton's idiosyncratic autobiography.
88. Mathias (1967), p. 106.
89. Ibid., p. 109.
90. Ibid., pp. 109–10.
91. Ibid., p. 114.
92. Ibid., p. 343.
93. Alec Waugh (1951), *The Lipton Story* (London: Cassell), p. 263.
94. Lewis (1938), p. 102.
95. Ian Lloyd (1978a), *Rolls-Royce: The Growth of a Firm* and (1978b) *Rolls-Royce: The Years of Endeavour* (London: Macmillan).
96. Lloyd (1978a), p. 93.
97. Ibid., p. 116.
98. Lewis (1938), p. 102.
99. Ibid., p. 101.
100. U.S. Department of Commerce, *Foreign Direct Investment in the United States*, vol. 3, Appendix A (Washington: GPO), p. 64.
101. Thomas R. Navin (1970), 'The 500 Largest American Industrials in 1917', *Business History Review*, vol. XLIV, no. 3.

NOTES TO CHAPTER 5: EIGHT CASE HISTORIES

1. The most important source of information is Charles Wilson (1954), *History of Unilever*, vol. 1 (London: Cassell). Original documents at Unilever House have also been consulted. See also *The Lever Story 1895–1959: Progress, Products, People* (1959), (London: Unilever Private Publication). D. K. Fieldhouse (1978), *Unilever Overseas* (London: Croom Helm) is concerned mainly with non-American expansion.
2. Nicholas Faith (1971), p. 57.
3. Christopher Tugendhat (1971), p. 35.
4. Faith (1971), pp. 56–7.

5. Wilson (1954), p. 99.
6. Faith (1971), p. 57.
7. The main reference used in this case history is D. C. Coleman (1969), *Courtaulds*, vol. II (Oxford: Clarendon Press). See also J. W. Markham (1952).
8. The main source for this case is Kendall Beaton (1951), *Enterprise in Oil* (New York: Appleton-Century-Crofts). See also Anthony Sampson (1975), *The Seven Sisters* (London: Hodder & Stoughton) and C. Tugendhat and A. Hamilton (1975). Also *A Short History of the Royal Dutch/Shell Group of Companies* (1975), Shell Centre, London. We are grateful to Mr Alan Peters for comments on an earlier draft and to Mr J. Boyajian of Shell Oil Company, U.S.A.
9. Drawn largely from W. J. Reader (1970), vol. I. Also Henry Wigglesworth, 'The Chemical Industries', in H. T. Warshaw (1928).
10. The main reference is Michael Sedgwick (1974), *Fiat* (London: Batsford). Also L. T. Wells, 'Automobiles', in R. Vernon (ed.) (1974), *Big Business and the State* (London: Macmillan).
11. The principal source is Reader (1970), Parts II and III.
12. The main source of information is J. Heer (1966), *World Events, 1866–1966. The First 100 Years of Nestlé* (Nestlé Alimentana S.A.). Also Nestlé and Anglo-Swiss Holding Company (1946), *This is Your Company*. We are also grateful for extensive comments on an earlier draft by executives of Nestlé Alimentana.
13. The main references are Georg Siemens (1957), *History of the House of Siemens* (Freiburg/Munich: Karl Alber), and particularly for European investments, J. D. Scott (1958), *Siemens Brothers, 1856–1958* (London: Weidenfeld & Nicolson).
14. Personal communication to authors from Werner-von-Siemens, Institute für Geschichte Des Hauses Siemens, München, dated 4 September 1978.
15. Seigfried von Werner and Herbert Goetzeler (1977), *The Seimens Company: Its Historical Role in the Progress of Electrical Engineering* (English version published by Siemens).
16. Personal communication cited in Note 14, dated 4 September 1978.
17. Ibid.

NOTES TO CHAPTER 6: CONCLUSION

1. J. H. Dunning (1961), p. 9.
2. J. W. Markham (1952), *Competition in the Rayon Industry* (Cambridge, Mass.: Harvard University Press).
3. Quoted in Markham (1952), p. 16.
4. Jeffrey S. Arpan and David A. Ricks (1979), *Directory of Foreign Manufacturers in the United States*, 2nd edition (Atlanta: Georgia State University).
5. Clark C. Spence (1958), *British Investments and the American Mining Frontier, 1860–1901* (New York: Cornell University Press) quote from p. 239.

6. Sasuly (1947).
7. Lewis (1938), p. 119.
8. Stopford (1974), quote from pp. 302–3.
9. Lewis (1938), p. 122.
10. See Ludwell Denny (1930), *America Conquers Britain: A Record of Economic War* (New York: Alfred A. Knopf).
11. See John Maurice Clark (1931), *The Costs of the War to the American People* (New Haven, Conn.: Yale University Press), and V. S. Clark (1929) vol. III. Improved production techniques were achieved after the spiriting away from Germany of four skilled dyestuffs chemists from Bayer in 1921. See Joseph Borkin (1979).
12. See Borkin (1979), particularly the chapter on 'Corporate Camouflage' for the full, fascinating and tortuous story.
13. Alice Teichova (1974), quote from p. 382.

Bibliography

Adler, Dorothy E. (1970), *British Investment in American Railways, 1834–1898* (Charlottesville: University Press of Virginia).
Alford, B. W. E. (1973), *W. D. and H. D. Wills and the Development of the U.K. Tobacco Industry, 1786–1965* (London: Methuen).
Arpan, Jeffrey S. and David A. Ricks (1979), *Directory of Foreign Manufacturers in the United States,* (2nd edition) (Atlanta: Georgia State University).
Bacon, Nathaniel T. (1900), 'American international indebtedness', *Yale Review,* November 1900.
Bain, Joe, S. (1951), 'Industrial Concentration and Anti-Trust Policy', in H. F. Williamson (ed.), *The Growth of the American Economy* (2nd edition) (Englewood Cliffs: Prentice-Hall).
Beaton, Kendall (1951), *Enterprise in Oil* (New York: Appleton-Century-Crofts).
Beer, J. J. (1959), *The Emergence of the German Dye Industry* (Urbana, Illinois: Illinois University Press).
Berill, Kenneth (1963), 'Foreign Capital and Take-Off', in W. W. Rostow (ed.), *The Economics of Take-Off into Sustained Growth* (London: Macmillan).
Bishop, J. Leander (1868), *A History of American Manufacturers, 1608–1860,* (3 volumes), reprinted 1966 (New York: Augustus Kelley).
Borkin, Joseph (1979), *The Crime and Punishment of I.G. Farben* (London: André Deutsch).
Brock, William R. (1973), *Conflict and Transformation, The United States, 1844–1877* (Harmondsworth: Pelican).
Brooke, Michael Z. and H. Lee Remmers (1970), *The Strategy of Multinational Enterprises* (London: Longman).
Buckley, Peter J. and Mark Casson (1976), *The Future of the Multinational Enterprise* (London: Macmillan).
Burgy, J. Herbert (1932), *The New England Cotton Textile Industry* (Baltimore: Waverly Press).
Burn, D. L. (1931), 'The Genesis of American Engineering Competition, 1850–1879', *Economic History,* vol. II, January 1931.
Buss, Dietrich G. (1976), 'Henry Villard: A Study of Transatlantic Investment and Interests, 1870–1895' (unpublished Ph.D. thesis, Claremont Graduate School).
Cairncross, Alec K. (1953), *Home and Foreign Investment, 1870–1913* (Cambridge: Cambridge University Press).
Clark, John Maurice (1931), *The Costs of the War to the American People* (New Haven, Conn.: Yale University Press).
Clark, Victor S. (1929), *History of Manufactures in the United States* (three volumes) (New York: McGraw-Hill).

Clements, Roger V. (1955a), 'British Investment and American Legislative Restrictions in the Trans-Mississippi West, 1880–1900', *Mississippi Valley Historical Review*, vol. XLII, September.
—— (1955b), 'The Farmers' Attitude Toward British Investment in American Industry', *Journal of Economic History*, vol. XV, no. 2.
Cochran, Thomas C. and William Miller (1942), *The Age of Enterprise* (New York: Macmillan).
Cole, Arthur Harrison (1926), *The American Wool Manufacture* (Cambridge, Mass.: Harvard University Press).
Coleman, D. C. (1969), *Courtaulds: An Economic and Social History* (Oxford: Clarendon Press).
Copeland, Melvin Thomas (1917), *The Cotton Manufacturing Industry of the United States* (New York: Augustus Kelley). Reprinted 1966.
Coram, T. C. (1967), 'The Role of British Capital in the Development of the United States, 1600–1914' (unpublished M.Sc. thesis, University of Southampton).
Corina, T. C. (1975), *Trust in Tobacco* (London: Michael Joseph).
Cottrell, P. L. (1975), *British Overseas Investment in the Nineteenth Century* (London: Macmillan).
Court, W. H. B. (ed.) (1965), *British Economic History, 1870–1914: Commentary and Documents* (Cambridge: Cambridge University Press).
Cramer, Clarence (1972), *American Enterprise: The Rise of U.S. Commerce* (London: Paul Elek).
Crapol, Edward P. (1973), *America for Americans: Economic Nationalism and Anglophobia in the Late Nineteenth Century* (Westport, Conn.: Greenwood Press).
Crutchley, G. W. (1921), *John Mackintosh: A Biography* (London: Hodder & Stoughton).
Davies, A. Emil (1926), *Foreign Investments* (London: A. W. Shaw).
Davis, J. S. (1917), *Essays in the Earlier History of American Corporations* (Cambridge, Mass.: Harvard University Press).
Denny, Ludwell (1930), *America Conquers Britain: A Record of Economic War* (New York: Alfred A. Knopf).
Dunning, John H. (1961), 'British Investment in U.S. Industry', *Moorgate and Wall Street*, Autumn.
—— (1970), *Studies in International Investment* (London: Allen & Unwin).
Edelstein, M. (1974), 'The Determinants of U.K. Industry Abroad, 1870–1913: The U.S. Case', *Journal of Economic History*, vol. 34, no. 4, December.
Faith, Nicholas (1971), *The Infiltrators* (London: Hamish Hamilton).
Feis, Herbert (1930), *Europe, The World's Banker, 1870–1914* (New Haven, Conn.: Yale University Press). (Reprinted 1961 for the Council on Foreign Relations).
Fieldhouse, D. K. (1978), *Unilever Overseas* (London: Croom Helm).
Fishlow, Albert (1965), *American Railroads and the Transformation of the Ante-Bellum Economy* (Cambridge, Mass.: Harvard University Press).
Franko, L. G. (1974), 'The Origins of Multinational Manufacturing by

Continental European Firms', *Business History Review*, vol. XLVIII, no. 3, Autumn.
—— (1976), *The European Multinationals* (London: Harper & Row).
Geigy, J. R., A.G. (undated), *200 Years Geigy* (Basel: J. R. Geigy A.G.).
Giddy, Ian H. (1978), 'The Demise of the Product Cycle Model in International Business Theory', *Columbia Journal of World Business*, vol. XIII, no. 1, Spring.
Glover, John G. and William B. Cornell (eds.) (1951), *The Development of American Industries* (3rd edition) (New York: Prentice-Hall).
Gras, N. S. B. and Henrietta M. Larson (1939), *Casebook in American Business History* (New York: F. S. Crofts).
Green, Constance McClauglin (1951), 'Light Manufactures and the Beginnings of Precision Manufacture', Chapter 11 of Harold F. Williamson (ed.), *The Growth of the American Economy* (2nd edition) (Englewood Cliffs: Prentice-Hall).
Green's of Wakefield (1956), *Waste Not: The Story of Green's Economiser* (London: Harley Publishing Co.).
Haber, L. F. (1958), *The Chemical Industry During the 19th Century* (Oxford: Clarendon Press).
—— (1971), *The Chemical Industry, 1900–1930* (Oxford: Clarendon Press).
Hall, A. R. (ed.) (1968), *The Export of Capital from Britain, 1870–1914* (London: Methuen).
Hazard, Blanche Evans (1921), *The Organisation of the Boot and Shoe Industry in Massachusetts before 1875* (Cambridge, Mass.: Harvard University Press).
Heer, Jean (1966), *World Events, 1866–1966. The First 100 Years of Nestlé* (Nestlé Alimentana, S.A.).
Hidy, Ralph W. (1941), 'The Organisation and Functions of Anglo-American Merchant Bankers, 1815–60', *Journal of Economic History*, December Supplement.
—— (1949), *The House of Baring in American Trade and Finance* (Cambridge, Mass.: Harvard University Press).
Hymer, Stephen H. (1976), *The International Operations of National Firms: A Study of Direct Foreign Investment* (Cambridge, Mass.: M.I.T. Press) (Previously an unpublished doctoral dissertation dating from 1960).
Jackson, W. Turrentine (1968), *The Enterprising Scot: Investors in the American West After 1873* (Edinburgh: Edinburgh University Press).
Jenks, Leland H. (1951), 'Britain and American Railway Development', *Journal of Economic History*, vol. XI, no. 4, Autumn.
—— (1971), *The Migration of British Capital to 1875* (London: Nelson). First published 1927.
Jeremy, David J. (1973), 'British Textile Technology Transmission to the United States: The Philadelphia Experience, 1770–1820', *Business History Review*, vol. XLVII, no. 1.
John, A. H. (1959), *A Liverpool Merchant House: Being the History of Alfred Booth and Company* (London: Allen & Unwin).
Johnson, Arthur M. and Barry E. Supple (1967), *Boston Capitalists and Western Railroads* (Cambridge, Mass.: Harvard University Press).

Bibliography

Jolly, W. P. (1976), *Lord Leverhulme: A Biography* (London: Constable).
Kaplan, A. D. H. (1964), *Big Enterprise in a Competition System* (revised edition) (Washington: The Brookings Institution).
Kindleberger, C. P. (1969), *American Business Abroad* (New Haven, Conn.: Yale University Press).
Knapp, John (1957), 'Capital Exports and Growth', *Economic Journal*, vol. LXVII, no. 3 (September) pp. 432–44.
Kuhlmann, Charles Byron (1929), *The Development of the Flour Milling Industry in the United States* (Boston: Houghton Mifflin).
Lenman, Bruce and Kathleen Donaldson (1971), 'Partners' Incomes, Investment and Diversification in the Scottish Linen Area, 1850–1921', *Business History*, vol. XIII, no. 1, January.
The Lever Story 1895–1959 (London: Unilever).
Levine, A. L. (1957), *Industrial Retardation in Britain, 1880–1914* (London: Weidenfeld & Nicolson).
Lewis, Cleona (1938), *America's Stake in International Investments* (Washington: The Brookings Institution).
Lipton, Thomas J. (1931), *Leaves from the Lipton Logs* (London: Hutchinson).
Lloyd, Ian (1978a), *Rolls-Royce: The Growth of a Firm* (London: Macmillan).
—— (1978b), *Rolls-Royce: The Years of Endeavour* (London: Macmillan).
Lytle, Richard H. (1968), 'The Introduction of Diesel Power into the United States, 1897–1912', *Business History Review*, vol. XLII, no. 2, Summer.
Mackintosh, Viscount Harold Vincent (1966), *By Faith and Work* (autobiography) (London: Hutchinson).
MacLaurin, W. Rupert (1949), *Invention and Innovation in the Radio Industry* (New York: Macmillan Inc.).
Markham, J. W. (1952), *Competition in the Rayon Industry* (Cambridge, Mass.: Harvard University Press).
Mathias, Peter (1967), *Retailing Revolution* (London: Longman).
—— (1969), *The First Industrial Nation* (London: Methuen).
McClain, D. S. (1974), 'Foreign Investment in U.S. Manufacturing and the Theory of Direct Investment' (unpublished doctoral thesis, Massachusetts Institute of Technology).
Morgan, E. Victor and W. A. Thomas (1962), *The Stock Exchange, its History and Functions* (London: Elek Books).
Morgan, H. Wayne (1971), *Unity and Culture: The United States, 1877–1900* (Harmondsworth: Pelican).
Navin, Thomas R. (1970), 'The 500 Largest American Industrials in 1917', *Business History Review*, vol. XLIV, no. 3.
Nelson, Ralph (1959), *Merger Movements in American Industry, 1895–1956* (Princeton, New Jersey: Princeton University Press).
Nestlé and Anglo-Swiss Holding Company (1946), *This is Your Company*.
North, Douglass (1960), 'The United States Balance of Payments, 1790–1860', in *Trends in the American Economy in the 19th Century* (Princeton, New Jersey: Princeton University Press).
—— (1963), 'Industrialisation in the United States', in W. W. Rostow

(ed.), *The Economics of Take-Off into Sustained Growth* (London: Macmillan).
Nurske, Ragnor (1954), 'The Problems of International Investment Today in the Light of 19th Century Experience', *Economic Journal*, vol. LXIV, no. 4, December.
Paish, G. (1911), 'Great Britain's Capital Investments in Individual Colonial and Foreign Countries', *Journal of the Royal Statistical Society*, vol. LXIV (January), pp. 167–200.
Paterson, Donald G. (1976), *British Direct Investment in Canada, 1870–1914: Estimates and Determinants* (Toronto: University of Toronto Press).
Pearce, W. M. (1964), *The Matador Land and Cattle Company* (Norman, Oklahoma: Oklahoma University Press).
Plummer, A. (1951), *International Combines in Modern Industry* (3rd edition) (London: Pitman).
Porter, Glenn and Harold C. Livesay (1971), *Merchants and Manufacturers* (Baltimore: Johns Hopkins Press).
Ragazzi, G. (1973), 'Theories of the Determinants of Direct Foreign Investments', *IMF Staff Papers*, vol. XX, no. 2, July.
Reader, W. J. (1970), *I.C.I.: A History* (Oxford: Oxford University Press).
Reckitt, Basil N. (1965), *The History of Reckitt and Sons Limited* (London: A. Brown & Sons).
Reddaway, W. B. et al. (1967 & 1968), *Effects of UK Direct Investment Overseas*, Interim and final reports (Cambridge: Cambridge University Press).
Richter, F. E. (1927), 'The Copper Mining Industry in the United States, 1845–1925', *Quarterly Journal of Economics*, vol. XLI, nos. 1 and 3, February and August.
Rippy, J. Fred (1955), 'British Investments in Texas Lands and Livestock', *Southwestern Historical Quarterly*, vol. LVIII, no. 1, January.
Rosenbloom, Arthur H. (1976), *Buying and Selling Businesses: The Past Shapes the Future* (New York: Standard Research Consultants).
Rostow, W. W. (ed.) (1963), *The Economics of Take-Off into Sustained Growth* (London: Macmillan).
Royal Institute of International Affairs (1937), *The Problem of International Investment* (Oxford: Oxford University Press).
Sampson, Anthony (1975), *The Seven Sisters* (London: Hodder & Stoughton).
Sasuly, Richard (1947), *I.G. Farben* (New York: Boni & Gaer).
Scott, J. D. (1958), *Siemens Brothers, 1858–1958* (London: Weidenfeld & Nicolson).
Sedgwick, M. (1974), *Fiat* (London: Batsford).
Shell U.K. (1975), *A Short History of the Royal Dutch/Shell Group of Companies* (London).
Siemens, G. (1957), *History of the House of Siemens* (Freiburg/Munich: Karl Alber).
Simpson, Colin (1972), *Lusitania* (Harmondsworth: Allen Lane).
Spence, Clark C. (1958), *British Investments and the American Mining*

Frontier, 1860–1901 (New York: Cornell University Press).
Staley, E. (1935), *War and the Private Investor* (Chicago: Chicago University Press).
Stampp, Kenneth M. (1966), *The Era of Reconstruction, 1865–77* (New York: Alfred A. Knopf).
Stapleton, Darwin, H. (1975), 'The Transfer of Technology to the United States in the Nineteenth Century' (unpublished Ph.D. thesis, University of Delaware).
Stopford, John M. (1974), 'The Origins of British-based Multinational Manufacturing Enterprises', *Business History Review*, vol. XLVIII, no. 3, Autumn.
—— (1976), 'Changing Perspectives on Investment by British Manufacturing Multinationals', *Journal of International Business Studies*, vol. 7, no. 2, Fall/Winter.
Supple, Barry E. (1963), *The Experience of Economic Growth* (New York: Random House).
—— (ed.) (1977), *Essays in British Business History* (Oxford: Oxford University Press).
Svedberg, Peter (1978), 'The Portfolio-Direct Composition of Private Foreign Investment in 1914 Revisited', *Economic Journal*, vol. 88, no. 4, December.
Teichova, Alice (1974), *An Economic Background to Munich: International Business and Czechoslovakia 1918–38* (Cambridge: Cambridge University Press).
Temin, Peter (1975), *Causal Factors in American Economic Growth in the Nineteenth Century* (London: Macmillan).
Tennant, Richard B. (1960), *The American Cigarette Industry* (New Haven, Conn.: Yale University Press).
Thistlethwaite, Frank (1963), 'From Wildcatting to Monopoly, 1850–1914' in Barry E. Supple (ed.), *The Experience of Economic Growth* (New York: Random House).
Thomas, Brinley (1967), 'The Historical Record of International Capital Movements to 1913' in J. H. Adler (ed.), *Capital Movements and Economic Development* (London: Macmillan). Reprinted in John H. Dunning (ed.) (1972), *International Investment* (Harmondsworth: Penguin).
Tischendorf, Alfred (1955), 'North Carolina and the British Investor, 1880–1910', *North Carolina Historical Review*, vol. XXXII, October.
Tugendhat, Christopher (1971), *The Multinationals* (London: Eyre & Spottiswoode).
—— and A. Hamilton (1975), *Oil, The Biggest Business* (London: Eyre Methuen).
Tyron, Rolla Milton (1917), *Household Manufactures in the United States, 1640–1860* (Chicago: University of Chicago Press).
United States Department of Commerce (1976), *Foreign Direct Investment in the United States* (nine volumes) (Washington, D.C.).
United States Department of Commerce, Bureau of the Census (1960), *Historical Statistics of the United States* (Washington, D.C.).

United States Federal Trade Commision (1919), *Report on the Meat Packing Industry* (Washington, D.C.).

Vernon, Raymond (1971), *Sovereignty at Bay* (London: Longman).

Von Werner, Seigfried and Herbert Goetzeler (1977), *The Siemens Company: Its Historical Role in the Progress of Electrical Engineering* (published by Siemens).

Ware, Caroline F. (1931), *The Early New England Cotton Manufacture* (New York: Russell & Russell).

Warshaw, H. T. (1928) (ed.), *Representative Industries in the United States* (London: Allen & Unwin).

Waugh, Alec (1951), *The Lipton Story* (London: Cassell).

Weber, Bernard and S. J. Handfield-Jones (1954), 'Variations in the Rate of Economic Growth in the U.S.A., 1869–1939', *Oxford Economic Papers*, vol. VI, no. 2, June.

Wells, Louis T. (1974), 'Automobiles', in Raymond Vernon (ed.), *Big Business and the State* (London: Macmillan).

Williamson, Harold F. (ed.) (1951), *The Growth of the American Economy* (2nd edition) (Englewood Cliffs: Prentice-Hall).

Wilson, Charles (1954), *The History of Unilever* (London: Cassell).

Woodruff, William (1966), *Impact of Western Man* (London: Macmillan).

Subject and name index

The term 'direct investment', unless qualified, refers to direct investment in the U.S.A. Similarly, 'exports' and 'imports', unless qualified, refer to exports from and imports to the U.S.A.

absentee landlords, 59–60
acquisitions, *see* mergers
advertising, 77–8, 89–90, 92
agents, 5, 23, 44, 65, 87, 91–2
agricultural industry, 32–3
aircraft engines, 80, 104
'Alien Land Acts' (1890's), 60
Alien Property Custodian, 14, 17, 35, 47, 50, 66, 123, 127–8
alkalis, 46, 105
    imports, 105
    production, 106
    tariffs, 105
'American Convention' (cartel), 102
American Dollar Securities Committee, 125
American Revolution, 21
Anglo-American War, 22
anti-trust policies, 28, 65
aspirin, 45
Australia
    direct investment in, 18, 24
    immigration, 11
    subsidiaries, 38
    tea industry, 78
Austria, direct investment, 14–16
automobile industry, *see* car industry

baby foods, 108
bacon, 77–8
Baker, D'A., 104
balance of payments, 12, 19, 124
banking and finance industry, 22–3, 70–2, 84
    foreign-owned companies, 70–3
bankruptcies, 40, 73
Bartikeit, E., 75
Beach, G., 75
Belgium
    capital exports, 12
    direct investment, 14–16, 34–5, 39, 85–6, 119–21

chemical and dyestuffs industry, 82
    oil industry, 51
    other industries, 81
belting, 75–6
Berliner, Dr., 113, 115
Bernhard, A. F., 92
bleaching powder, 46
boiler industry, 37
bonds, *see* securities
brewing industry, 4, 15, 27, 53–6
    company failures, 55
    foreign-owned companies, 54–5
    prohibition, 53–4
    syndicate investment, 54
British Companies Act (1862), 22
business history, research, xii

Canada
    direct investment, 81
    direct investment by U.S.A., 26
    immigration, 11
    subsidiary companies, 38
    tea industry, 78
capital exports, 3, 11–19
    colonial times to 1800, 20–1
    1800 to Civil War, 22–3
    Civil War to World War I, 24–30
    see also country names
capital markets, 7, 28
car industry, 68–9, 96, 103–5
    competition, 104
    gearboxes, 76
    imports, 68, 103–4
    mergers, 79
    product differentiation, 83, 104
    return on investment, 104–5
    sales, 100, 104
    subsidiaries, 103–4
    tyres, 76
carpet industry, 50
cartels, 5, 83

Germany, 44
   see also company names, industry names
cattle industry, 15, 27, 59, 60–1, 84
cement industry, 80
Ceylon, 78
cheese, 77
chemical and dyestuffs industry, 44–7
   artificial dyestuffs, 44–5
   cartels, 45–6, 106
   competition, 105–6
   foreign-owned companies, 82–3, 120
   mergers, 47, 106–7
   patents, 105, 107
   tariffs, 45–6, 83, 105–6, 127
   technological innovation, 105
   technology transfer, 46–7
chlorates, 47
Civil War, 61
Clark, G. A., 48
Clayton Act (1914), 28
clothing, 50
Cobden Treaty (1860), 67
Cogswell, W. B., 46, 106
companies
   case histories, 85–118
   history, 20–2
   failures, 23, 38, 121
   growth, 8–9, 22–3, 73–4
   management structures, 28, 41, 78–9, 121
   see also company names, industry names
competition, 6, 83
   chemical and dyestuffs industry, 105–6
   explosives industry, 102
   oil industry, 28, 51, 53, 100
   soap industry, 87
   tobacco industry, 28, 64
condensed milk, 108
confectionery industry, 38
confiscation of assets, *see* Alien Property Custodian
   see also Germany, industry names
co-operatives, 75
copper industry, 57
corporate planning, 128
cotton industry, 83
Countway, F. A., 89, 92
currency system, 25
cutlery industry, 50
cyanides, 47

Denmark, 80
dental supplies, 80

depressions, 23
Deterding, H., 95–6
developing countries, 13
Dingley Tariff (1897), 8, 46, 50, 105
direct investment, 119–21
   by country, 119–21
   by historical periods, 20–42
   by industry, 15, 120–21, 123
   effects of World War I, 116–17, 123–8
   extent of, 119, 121–2, 127
   foreign-owned companies, 82–3, 120–21
      failures, 121
   forms of, 3, 116–17, 121
   impact of, 121–3, 128–9
      on balance of payments, 12, 19, 124
   investment cycles, 18–19, 26
   motives for, 5–7, 83, 118–19
   return on investment, 7–8, 40, 89–91, 94, 116–17
   technological innovations, 83, 118, 122
   see also capital exports, *company names, country names, industry names*
direct investment other than in U.S.A., 116–18
   see also company names, country names, industry names
distribution, 23, 92
diversification, 6
drugs, 45
Duke, J. B., 64–5
dyestuffs industry, *see* chemical and dyestuffs industry
dynamite, 101
   see also explosives industry
dynamos, 114

'Eagle' (brand), 80, 108
East Germany, *see* Germany
Eckmeyer, G., 65
electrical industry, 67–8, 112–15
   confiscation of assets, 68
   foreign-owned companies, 68, 112
   mergers, 112–14
   patents, 113–14
   technological innovations, 68, 114
entrepreneurs, 3, 22, 76–9
Erie Canal, 23
Europe
   capital exports, 12
   direct investment, 16–17, 23
   direct investment by U.S.A., 26

Index

emigration, 11
labour force, 30
explosives industry, 100–2
   cartels, 102
   competition, 102
   foreign-owned companies, 101
   mergers, 101
   patents, 101
   tariffs, 127
exports, *see company names, industry names*

family firms, 73
finance, *see* banking and finance industry
flax, 47
flour milling industry, 63
food industry, 76, 107–12
   brands, 108–9
   competition, 108–9, 111
   imports, 108
   mergers, 108
   tariffs, 108, 110–11
footwear industry, 48, 73–4
foreign exchange, 24
France
   capital exports, 12
   direct investment, 14–17, 34–5, 39, 119–21
      metal industry, 66
      oil industry, 51, 82
      other industries, 81
   imports from U.S.A., 74
Franco-German War (1870–1), 114

gearboxes, 76
Germany
   capital exports, 12, 24
   confiscation of assets, 126–7
   direct investment, 14–17, 34–5, 82, 85–6, 119–21
      brewing industry, 54
      car industry, 68–9
      chemical and dyestuffs industry, 44–7
      electrical industry, 67–8, 112–15
      explosives industry, 101–2
      metals industry, 65–6
      textile industry, 50
   imports from U.S.A., 74
glass industry, 126
   colonial times to 1800, 20–1
gloves, 74
gold rush, 23, 57
government incentives, 6
government securities
   direct investment by U.K., 13, 18, 25

Granger Movement, 59
gross national product, 33, 121–3, 128–9

Halske, J. G., 113
ham, 77–8
Hazard, R., 106
hides and skins, *see* leather industry
historical periods
   colonial times to 1800, 20–1
   1800 to the Civil War, 22–3
   Civil War to World War I, 24–30
Holland
   capital exports, 12
   direct investment, 14–16, 34–5, 85–6, 119–21
      banking and finance industry, 71–2
      oil industry, 51, 82
Hope, H., 75
horizontal integration, 9
hosiery industry, 50
hours of work, 75
Hungary
   direct investment, 14–16

immigration, 11, 24, 32, 50
import controls, *see* tariffs
imports, *see company names, industry names*
incomes, 32–3
India, direct investment in, 18
Indo-European Telegraph Line, 114
industrial development, 28
industries, *see industry names*
innovations, *see* technological innovations
insurance industry, 71–2
   foreign-owned companies, 72
inventions, *see* technological innovations
investment cycles, 18–19, 26
investors' control, 2
iron industry, 21, *see also* metal industry, steel industry
Italy
   direct investment, 34–5
      car industry, 68, 103–5

jobbers, *see* agents
joint ventures, 27–8, 38, 116–18, 121
   see also company names
Johnson, C., 79–80

labour force
   shortages, 30, 80, 93
   welfare, 98, 100
lace industry, 50

land development industry, 15, 27, 59–63, 84
  absentee landlords, 59–60
  banking and finance industry, 70–1
  company failures, 59–61
  foreign-owned companies, 59–61
  syndicate investment, 59, 61
leather industry, 73–4
  company failures, 73
  exports, 74
  salesmen, 74
  tariffs, 73
  technological innovations, 74
Leblanc process, 31, 46, 107
legislation
  'Alien Land' Acts (1890s), 60
  British Companies Act (1862), 22
  Clayton Act (1914), 28
  Morill Act (1861), 8
  Sherman Act (1890), 28, 97
Lever, W. H., (first Viscount Leverhulme), 86–7, 90
licencees, 5
'Lifebuoy' (brand), 87–8, 91–2
linen industry, 50
Lipton, T. J., 76–9
liquor industry, see brewing industry
Longeloth, J., 66
'Lux' (brand), 89
Luxembourg, direct investment, 34

McKinley Tariff (1892), 8, 46, 67, 105
management structures, 28, 41, 78–9, 121
man-made fibres industry, 82, 93–5
  cartels, 94
  foreign-owned companies, 93
  patents, 93–4
  tariffs, 93
manufacturing industry
  direct investment, 30
  output, 32–3
  productivity, 30
  see also company names, industry names
markets
  imperfections of, 7–8, 119
  internalisation, 8–9
'Marlboro' (brand), 65
market economy, development of, 27–9, 32–3
match industry, 62
meat packing, 77–8

mergers, 28
  see also company names, industry names
metal industry, 65–6
  confiscation of assets, 66
  subsidiaries, 66
Meysenburg, Mr, 113
Miller, V., 104
mining industry, 15, 18, 27, 56–8
  company failures, 57–8
  foreign-owned companies, 56–8
  portfolio investment, 56
  speculation, 56–7
  syndicate investment, 56
  technological innovation, 57
'Monkey' (brand), 87
monopolies, 5
Morill Act (1861), 8
mortgages, see banking and finance industry
Most Noble Order of the Knights of Labour, 75
multinational companies, 9, 28, 38, 128

Napoleonic Wars, 22
naval stores industry, 21
Netherlands, see Holland
New Zealand, immigration, 11
Nobel, A., 100–2

oil industry, 15, 50–3, 83, 95–100
  advertising, 100
  competition, 28, 51, 53, 100
  exports, 51, 95–6
  foreign-owned companies, 52
  imports, 51, 97
  marketing, 53
  mergers, 51, 95–6
  oil tankers, 95, 98
  patents, 97
  pipelines, 97–8
  price cutting, 96, 100
  refining, 97–8
  vertical integration, 96, 98, 100
oligopoly, 28, 119

Page, D., 109
Page, F., 109
Page, G., 108–9
paint industry, 79
patents, 5, 9, 118–19, 123
  infringements, 40
Payne–Aldrich Tariffs (1909), 93
Pettit, S. W., 93

phenacetin, 45
phosphorus, 46
population, 32
Populist Movement, 59
portfolio investment, 1–4, 12, 24
pottery industry, 30
product failures, 38
   see also company names
production costs, 83
prohibition, 53–4
property industry, *see* land development industry, real estate industry
protectionism, *see* tariffs
Provident Fund, 98, 100
public opinion, 5
public utilities, direct investment by U.K., 13

quotas, *see* tariffs

radio industry, *see* telecommunications industry
railway industry, 13, 15, 18, 22, 24–5
   mergers, 28
   portfolio investment, 69–70
   securities, 69
raw materials, 6, 9, 83, 92
   costs, 89
rayon, 49, 94, 122
real estate industry, 15
Republican Party, 65
retailing, 77–9
   advertising, 77–8
return on investment, *see* company names, direct investment
'Rinso' (brand), 89
risk, *see* company names, direct investment
Rockefeller, J. D., 95, 97
Roosevelt, F. O., 41
Roosevelt, T., President, 65
Rothschild family, 57, 95

salesmen, 74, 87–9
Samuel, M., 95
'Scandinavia' (brand), 75
Scotland, direct investment, 72
securities, 3
   direct investment by U.K., 14, 22, 69
Sherman Act (1890), 28, 97
shipbuilding industry, colonial times to 1800, 21
shipping industry, 73–5
   oil tankers, 95, 98

Shoeleather Association of Manufacturers, 75
shoes, *see* footwear industry
Siegle, G., 44
Siemens, Werner, 113–14
Siemens, William, 114
silk industry, 50, 67
   immigrant workers, 67
   tariffs, 67
slavery, abolition of, 30
small business, 21
soap industry, 46, 76, 86–93
   competition, 87
   direct investment, 90–1
   foreign-owned companies, 87
   patents, 89
   portfolio investment, 90
   raw materials, 89, 92
   tariffs, 86, 90
   see also company names
soda, 46, 105
   production, 106
sodium, 47
South Africa, tea industry, 78
South African War, 26
South America, immigration, 11
Southern States, 23, 25
spirits industry, *see* brewing industry
steel industry, 66
Stiegel, Baron, 21
stocks, *see* securities
subsidiary companies, 3, 29
   foreign-owned, 34–41, 82, 118
Suez Canal, 95
sugar, 109
'Sunlight' (brand), 76, 87–8, 91
surgical instruments, 80
'Surpass' (brand), 74
strikes, 75
Sweden, direct investment, 35, 86
Switzerland
   capital exports, 12
   direct investment, 14–16, 34–5, 82, 85, 119–21
   chemical and dyestuffs industry, 44
   food industry, 76
syndicate investment, 4, 27
   see also industry names

takeovers, *see* mergers
tallow, 88
tanning, *see* leather industry

tariffs, 5
  1842, 23
  1870–1917, 2, 7–8, 25, 38, 118–19
  see also industry names, tariff names
tea industry, 76, 78
  advertising, 78
  Canada, 78
  retailing, 78
  South Africa, 78
technological innovations, 83, 118, 122
  see also company names, industry names
technology transfer, 9, 12–13, 21, 24, 30–1, 122–3
  legislation against, 21
  see also industry names
telecommunications industry, 33, 40–1, 114
Tennant, C., 101
textile industry, 23, 47–50, 83
  confiscation of assets, 50
  lace industry, 50
  man-made fibres, 82, 93–4
  mergers, 48
  tariffs, 50
  technology transfer, 30
thread, 48–9
timber industry, 62
tin-plate industry, 67
  tariffs, 67
tobacco industry, 64–5
  brands, 65
  colonial times to 1800, 21
  competition, 28, 64
  mergers, 64
  trusts, 64–5
trade unions, 75
transport costs, 5, 83
transport system, 23
  see also water transport
Treiber, C., 75
trusts, 45
  see also company names
Turkey, direct investment, 14–16
tyres, 76

United Kingdom
  capital exports, 12, 21, 24, 126
  direct investment, 12–16, 22, 27, 29, 82, 85–6, 119–21, 125
  banking and finance industry, 70–3
  brewing industry, 53–5
  car industry, 68
  flour milling industry, 63
  government securities, 13, 18, 25
  land development industry, 59–62
  metal industry, 66
  mining industry, 56–8
  oil industry, 51, 98
  other countries, 126
  other industries, 81
  paint industry, 79
  public utilities, 13
  railway industry, 69–70
  raw materials, 13
  securities, 14, 22, 69
  textile industry, 50
  tin-plate industry, 67
  tobacco industry, 64–5
Usher, G., 37
U.S.S.R., exports, 74

velvet, 49
vertical integration, 9, 62, 79
  see also oil industry
Villard, H., 112

washing machines, 89
water transport, 23
'Welcome' (brand), 87–8
West Germany, *see* Germany
wheat market, 63
Whitney's gin, 30
wholesalers, *see* agents
window frames, 75
wool industry, 49–50
World War I, 1n
  effects on direct investment, 116–17, 123–8

Company name index

AEG, 68, 85–6, 112, 117
Alabama Coal, Iron, Land and
    Colonization, 59–60
Alabama Great Southern Railway, 70
Alabama Traction, Light and Power, 81
Alaska United, 58
Albright and Wilson, 37, 46
Allied Chemical and Dye, 106–7
Aluminium, 47
American Freehold-Land Mortgage,
    70–1
American Gasoline, 51, 97
American Life Assurance and Trust, 72
American Metal, 17, 57, 66
American Pastoral, 61
American Sales Book, 81
American Smelting and Refining, 126
American Thread, 48–9, 81
American Tin Plate, 67
American Tobacco, 28, 64
American Velvet, 67
American Viscose, 29, 82, 93–4, 120, 122
Anaconda, 57
Anglo-American Provision, 59
Anglo-Swiss Condensed Milk, 7, 34, 76, 85–6, 107–12, 117
    growth, 108
    imports, 108
    mergers, 108–11
    return on investment, 108–9, 112, 118, 121
    subsidiaries in U.K., 108–9, 111
    subsidiaries in U.S.A., 108–10
    tariffs, 108, 110
Arizona Consolidated Copper Mines, 58
Arizona Copper, 58
Armour, 77–8, 88
Asiatic Petroleum, 96
Atlantic and Great Western Railway, 69
Atlantic Giant Powder, 101
Atlantis Sales, 36
Austro-Fiat, 104

Badishe, 47
Balfour, Williamson, 97

Bank of England, 125
Bank of North America, 72
Barbour, W. & Sons, 47
Barbour Flax, 47
Baring Bank, 22, 26, 70
Barrett, 106
Bartholomay Brewing, 55
BASF, 31, 127
Bayer, 34–5, 44–5, 127
Beer Sondheimer, 66
Belgian-Bohemian Mining, 39, 57
Berlin, 47
Berlitz, 34, 80
Bethlehem Steel, 28
Booth, A., 73–5
Booth Steamship, 73
Borax Consolidated, 57–8
Borden, 34, 108
Bosch, 34–5
Bosch Magneto, 68
Boston Consolidated Gold and Copper
    Mining, 57
Boston Thread and Twine, 48
Botany, 50
Botany Worsted Mills, 17
Bradford Dyers Association, 39, 49
British American Insurance, 71
British–American Tobacco, 64
British Belting and Asbestos, 76
British Dynamite, 101
British Otis Steel, 66
British Portland Cement, 79
Brooke, B., 76, 87
Brown and Williamson, 65
Brunner, Mond, 105–7
Bryant & May, 62
Burroughs Wellcome, 75
Butte County Railroad, 62

Cadahy, 88
California Pastoral and Agricultural, 61
Californian Oilfields, 51, 97
Camp Bird, 58
Capital Freehold Land and Investment, 60
Cash, J. & J., 49, 83

154 Index

Cassella, 47
Chemical Works of Buffalo, 44
Chicago Breweries, 55
Cincinnati Breweries, 55
City of Chicago Brewing and Malting, 55
Clark, J. & J., 48
Clark Mile-end, 48
Claudish Ash, 39
Coats, J. & P., 27, 36, 39, 48
Coats & Clark, 48−9, 123
Cobbett, W. W., 75
Colgate, 88
Compagnie Continentale Edison, 114
Conant Thread, 48
Consolidated Tobacco, 64
Continental Tobacco, 64
Cook, F. W., Brewing, 53, 55
Cook, T., 72
Cooke, J., 23
Cork Packing House, 77
Courtaulds, 27, 29, 32, 36, 38, 49−50, 82−3, 85−6, 91, 93−5, 116
    cartels, 94
    imports, 93−4
    patents, 93−4
    return on investment, 94
    subsidiaries in U.S.A., 93−4, 120
Crescent Mining, 58
Cressbrook Dairy, 111
Curtis, Davis, 76, 86−7

Daimler Benz, 34−5, 68
Degussa, 34−5, 47
De Lamar Mining, 57−8
Delta & Pine Land, 39
Densten Felt and Hair, 74−5
Dentists Supply, 80
Denver United Breweries, 55
De Trey, 80
Deutsche Edison, 112
De Witt & Hertz, 68, 80
Diamond Match, 62
Dick, R. & J., 75, 81
Ducktown Sulphur, Copper and Iron, 57−8
Duesenberg Motors, 104
Dundee, 51
Dunlop Pneumatic Tyre, 38, 76
Dunlop Tire and Rubber, 76
Dupont, E. I., 28, 102
Dynamit-Aktiengesellschaft, 101

Edison General Electric, 68, 112, 114
Eiseman Magneto, 68

English Condensed Milk, 108
English Electric, 114
English Petroleum and Mining, 50
English Sewing Cotton, 27, 36, 48
Exploration, 57

Fel, 88
Fiat, 34, 68, 86, 103−5, 116
    imports, 103−4
    subsidiaries in Austria, 104−5
    subsidiaries in U.K., 104
    subsidiaries in U.S.A., 103−4
Fiat Motors, 104
Fine Cotton Spinners and Doublers Association, 39, 59
Finlayson Bousfield, 48
Fleming, R., Bank, 72
Ford, H., 76
Forestal Land, Timber and Railways, 39
Forstmann and Huffmann, 49−50
Fowler, G. & Son, 59
Fownes Brothers, 81
Fremont Oil, 51−2
French, R. T., 36
French American Banking, 71
Frontenac Consolidated Mines, 58
Fuel Economiser, 37
Fussell, 111

Galak Condensed Milk, 111
Gardiner−Lucas Glue and Gelatine, 74
Geigy, 34, 35, 45
Genasco Silk Works, 93
General Aniline and Film, 47
General Artificial Silk, 49
General Chemical, 106
General Electric, 28, 68
German-American Lumber, 17
German Powder Group, 102
Giant Powder, 101
Girard Bank, 72
Glasgow and Western Exploration, 39
Goebel Brewing, 55
Grant Locomotives, 113
Greens of Wakefield, 37
Gulf Oil, 95, 98

Hamburg-American Line Terminal and Navigation, 17
Handsworth Land and Cattle, 61
Harmsworth, McKay, Irons, 60
Hayden, 47
Hirsh, A. & Son, 17, 66
Hoechst, 31, 45, 47

Hollander and Tangeman, 103
Holliday, T., 44
Howard & Bullock, 37
Hudson River Aniline Works, 44

ICI, 107
IG Farben, 47
IG Farben Trust, 45, 127
Imperial Tobacco, 64
Indian Refining, 96
Indian Thread Mills, 48
Indianapolis Breweries, 55
International Paints, 79
Investment Co. for Electrical Enterprises, 71

Johnstone Packing, 77
Jones, F., Brewing, 55
Jualin Alaska Mine, 39, 57
Jurgens, 31

Kalle, 47
Kammgarnspinnere, Stoehrond, 50
Kannecott Copper, 66
Kansas, Oklahoma Oil and Refining, 51–2
Kellys Directories, 39
Kent and Stevens, 73
Kern River Oilfields of California, 51–2
Kerr and Clark Thread, 48
Knox, W. J., 48
Kny-Scherer, 17, 80
Kohler and Peter, 111–12
Kuttroff, Pickhardt, 44

Lamont, Corliss, 88, 111
Land Mortgage Bank of Texas, 71
Landenburgh, Thalmann, 66
Levassor, 68
Lever Brothers, 7, 27, 36, 43, 76, 81, 83, 85–93, 116, 123
  advertising, 89–90, 92
  agents, 87, 91–2
  brands, 87, 89, 91
  competition, 88
  employees, 90
  imports, 87
  marketing, 88–9, 92
  new products, 89
  reasons for direct investment, 86
  return on investment, 89–91, 118, 121
  sales methods, 87, 91
  subsidiaries in U.S.A., 87–9
  subsidiaries overseas, 91–2

Liggett & Meyers, 28
Linen Thread, 39, 48
Lipton, T. J., 78, 93
Lipton Packing, 77
Liverpool, London & Globe Insurance, 71
Lloyds Bank, 72
Lorillard, P., 28
Loring, A. C., 63
Lowenstein, 74
Lustre Fibres, 94

Mackintosh, 37–8
Manhattan Bank, 72
Marconi Wireless Telegraph, 38–41, 79
Margarine Uni, 34–5, 80
Marshall, 48
Massey-Harris Harvester, 81
Matador Land and Cattle, 60–1
Mathieu, J. P., 74
Mellon, 95, 98
Mercedes, 103
Merchant Exchange, 70
Merck, 17, 47
Merton, 66
Metallgesellschaft, 34–5, 66, 127
Meyer Packing House, 77
Michelin, A., 34, 39, 76
Midwest Refining, 51, 125
Milwaukee and Chicago Breweries, 55
Minerals Separation, 58
Missouri Land, 60
Monarch Knitting, 81
Morell, 39
Morgan Crucible, 79
Morse Brothers, 36
Mortgage & Debenture, 71
Mount Carbon, 60
Mountain Copper, 58
Murphy, M., 58

National Aniline and Chemical, 106
Natomas, 58
Nestlé, H., 27, 35, 76, 83, 85–6, 108–12, 117
  mergers, 109–11
  return on investment, 112
  subsidiaries in Australia, 111
  subsidiaries in Germany, 110
  subsidiaries in Norway, 110
  subsidiaries in Spain, 110
  subsidiaries in U.K., 110
  subsidiaries in U.S.A., 110
  tariffs, 110–11

New England Breweries, 55
New York Breweries, 55
New York City Freehold Estates, 60
New York Life Assurance and Trust, 71
New York Taxi Cab, 34, 80–1
Newall, 113
Niagara Electrochemical, 34, 47
Niagara Falls Power, 47
Nobel, A., 101
Nobel and Nobel Explosives Trust, 85–6, 100–3, 116
   joint ventures, 101–2
   mergers, 101–2
   patents, 101
   return on investment, 103, 121
   subsidiaries in U.S.A., 101–2
Nobel Dynamite Trust, 101–2
Nobel's Explosives, 101–2
North American Chemical, 47
North American Land & Timber, 60
Northern Assurance, 71
Norwegian Milk Condensing, 110

Ogden, 64
Ohio Life Assurance & Trust, 72
Oklahoma Oil and Refining, 51–2
Oldbury Electrochemical, 46
Olympic Portland Cement, 57, 79, 81
Orange County Milk Association, 108
Oregon Mortgage, 70–1
Oregon Railway, 69
Oroville Dredging, 58
Otis Steel, 57, 81

Pacific Loan and Investment, 71
Pacific Oilfields, 52
Panhard, 68, 103
Pechiney, 34
Pepsodent, 93
Phelps Dodge, 58
Philadelphia and Reading, 70
Philip Morris, 65
Phoenix Insurance, 71
Pierce-Arrow, 79
Pillsbury Flour Mills, 63
Pillsbury-Washburn Flour Mills, 63, 81
Platte Land, 60
Plymouth Consolidated Gold Mines, 58
Prairie Cattle, 59, 61
Premier Petroleum, 52
Prescott, 36
Procter & Gamble, 88–9
Pure Oil, 51, 125

Railroads Lands, 39
Rathbone, 73
Reckitt and Sons, 36
Renault, 103
Republic Steel, 28
Reynolds, R. J., 28
Riordan, 81
Riverside Orange, 60
Roessler & Hasslacher Chemical Co., 17, 34, 47
Rolls Royce, 39, 68, 79–80
Rolls Royce of America, 79
Rosengarten and Sons, 47
Roxana Petroleum, 52, 97–8
Royal Dutch, 95–6
Royal Dutch Shell, 27, 34, 36, 51, 86, 95–100, 116, 118
   employee welfare, 98, 100
   exports, 95
   history, 95
   imports, 97
   marketing, 96
   mergers, 95–6
   patents, 97
   pipelines, 97
   refining, 97
   subsidiaries in U.S.A., 97, 123
      financial performance, 99
   subsidiaries overseas, 96–7
   vertical integration, 98, 100
Rugby Tennessee, 60

St John Mines, 58
St Louis Breweries, 54–5
Salt, T., 49
San Antonio Land, 60
San Francisco Breweries, 55
San Jacinto Land, 60
Santa Maria Oilfields, 52
Scandinavia Belting, 75
Scandinavian Condensed Milk, 109
Schering, 47
Schoellkopf Aniline, 44
Schoenhofer, P., Brewing, 17
Scottish American Mortgage, 59, 71
Seabord Oil, 97
Seifenpulver, 92
Semet-Solvay, 81
Shell of California, 51–2
Shell Transport and Trading, 51, 53, 83
Siemens, W., 113
Siemens & Halske, 27, 34–5, 68, 80, 85–6, 112–15, 117
   company failures, 114–15, 121

mergers, 113–14
patents, 114–15
return on investment, 115
subsidiaries in U.K., 113–14
subsidiaries in U.S.A., 112–13
subsidiaries in U.S.S.R., 114
technological innovations, 114
Siemens & Halske Electric, 112–13
Siemens Brothers, 113–14
Siemens Brothers Dynamo Works, 114
Siemens Frères, 114
Silverfields, 58
S.K.F., 35, 80
Smidth, F. L., 80
Solvay, 27, 31, 34–5, 46–7, 81, 83, 86, 105–7, 117
   joint ventures, 106–7
   market share, 106
   mergers, 106
   patents, 105, 107
   return on investment, 107
   subsidiaries in U.K., 107
   subsidiaries in U.S.A., 106, 120
   technological innovation, 105
Solvay Process, 106
Southern Aluminium, 58, 66, 125
Southern and Illinois Central Railway, 70
Southern Pacific Railroad, 62
Southern States Coal, Iron and Land, 56, 66
Springfield Breweries, 55
Standard Chartered Bank, 72
Standard Explosive, 102
Standard Oil, 28–9, 45, 51, 53, 83, 98, 100, 118
   mergers, 95
Standard Oil Trust, 51, 97
Steinway, 68
Sterling Coal, 58
Sterling Trust, 39

Sterling Drug, 45
Strattons Independence, 58
Surpass Leather, 74–5
Swan Land & Cattle, 61
Swift, 59, 88

Telefunken, 41
Texas Land Mortgage, 70–1
Texas Oilfields, 51
Thomson Houston, 68, 112
Tom Boy Gold Mines, 57–8
Trumble, 97
Trust and Mortgage of Iowa, 60
Tuck, R., & Sons, 39

Unilever, 79, 123
Union dès Pétroles d'Oklahoma, 51–2, 125
Union Electric, 68
United Alkali, 37, 47
United Cigar Stores, 28
United Railway & Trading, 60
United States Brewing, 17
United States Lumber & Cotton, 60
United Wireless, 40
U.S. Blasting Oil, 101
U.S. Steel, 28, 45
U.S. Trust, 39
Utah Copper, 57, 66

Valley Pipe Line, 97
Vibro Syndicate, 58
Viscose, 49
Vogelstein, L., 17, 66

Wah Chang Mining & Smelting, 58
Warner, H. H., 81
Washington, 55
Watts Iron and Steel, 57, 66
Westquarter Chemical, 101
Williams Harvey, 39